FALCONS AND HAWKS

Great Creatures of the World

FALCONS AND HAWKS

Facts On File

New York • Oxford • Sydney

Written by Dr Penny Olsen
Consultant: Dr Ian Newton

About the author
Penny Olsen's home is a 16 hectare (40 acre) farm
just outside of Canberra, Australia's capital city. It is
far from an ordinary farm; the only livestock are
Louie, her 28-year-old horse, and about 40 hawks,
eagles and falcons.
   Dr Olsen has been studying hawks and owls in the
field since 1975, particularly the Peregrine Falcon.
She has written more than 50 scientific papers and
many magazine articles, and has contributed to
several books, most recently to *Birds of Prey*. She has
also been involved in making documentaries for TV.

Facts On File, Inc.   Facts On File Limited
460 Park Avenue South   Collins Street
New York NY 10016   Oxford OX4 1XJ
USA   United Kingdom

Library of Congress Cataloging in Publication data
is available on request from Facts On File.

Facts On File books are available at special discounts
when purchased in bulk quantities for businesses,
associations, institutions or sales promotions. Please
contact the Special Sales Department of our New
York office at 212/683-2244 (dial 800/322-8755
except in NY, AK or HI).

Produced by Weldon Owen Pty Limited
43 Victoria Street, McMahons Point NSW 2060,
Australia
Telex AA23038, Fax (02) 929 8352
A member of the Weldon International
Group of Companies
Sydney • London • Paris • San Francisco

Chairman: Kevin Weldon
President: John Owen
General Manager: Stuart Laurence
Publisher: Alison Pressley
Project Coordinator: Beverley Barnes
Co-editions Editor: Derek Barton
Copy Editor: Beverley Barnes
Editorial Assistant: Veronica Hilton
Illustrations: Tony Pyrzakowski
Designer: Diane Quick
Production Director: Mick Bagnato
Production Assistant: Simone Perryman

Typeset by Post Typesetters, Brisbane, Queensland
Printed by Kyodo Printing Co. (Singapore) Pty Ltd
Printed in Singapore

A WELDON OWEN PRODUCTION

*Page 1: Birds of prey hunt other animals. Here, a Rough-legged Buzzard has returned to the nest
with a vole for her chicks.*

*Page 2: Two squabbling Eurasian Buzzards strike at each other with feet and talons, their most
powerful weapons.*

Page 5: The keen eye and hooked beak of this Red-tailed Hawk are typical of birds of prey.

David E. Rowley/Planet Earth Pictures

Contents

Opposite page: Can you spot the Australian Kestrel perched on this huge cliff?

What is a bird of prey?

Birds of prey have hooked beaks for tearing flesh and powerful feet with sharp, curved talons for catching prey. They are strong-winged, powerful fliers, with very good eyesight. For thousands of years these qualities have fascinated humans.

Daytime meat-eaters

Most birds of prey, unlike owls, hunt in the daytime. They eat animals, either found dead or captured alive. Some are specialized hunters; for example, the Honey Buzzard lives on honeycomb and grubs, and the Snail Kite eats mostly large water snails. Others are generalists; the versatile Brown Falcon will eat insects, birds, rabbits, shrimps, and many other creatures, found dead or alive. The specialists live only where they can find enough of their special food, but the generalists are able to live over a much wider area.

Birds of prey are found on every continent except Antarctica, and on many islands far out in the ocean. They live in treeless deserts and dense rainforests; high mountains and low-lying swamplands; wilderness and cities. The number of types of birds of prey in a particular area varies. In general, you find more species,

> ## Some facts and figures
> There are about 292 different species, or types, of birds of prey. They can be divided into four groups of closely related species, known as families: **Cathartidae**, vultures that are related to storks (seven species); **Accipitridae**, kites, harriers, hawks, eagles, the Osprey, and vultures that are related to hawks (lots of species, about 224); **Sagittariidae**, the Secretary-bird (only one species); and **Falconidae**, falcons, falconets and caracaras (about 60 species).

▼ *A Brahminy Kite glides effortlessly above the forest. Humans have always admired the freedom and power of such birds of prey. The kite is sacred to followers of the Hindu religion; they believe it carries the god Vishnu.*

or types, closer to the equator than in temperate climates. Only four species breed in the high Arctic, but a hundred or more species breed in tropical forests around the world.

Birds of prey and humans

Birds of prey have long been admired for their beauty and powers of flight. Some are trained to hunt for human enjoyment. At the same time, they are persecuted by humans and blamed for killing livestock or game animals favored by hunters. A few birds of prey have become very rare because humans have destroyed their habitat.

Falcons and hawks

Birds of prey are also known as raptors. There are many types of raptors. This book, *Falcons and Hawks*, deals with falcons, caracaras, kites, harriers, hawks, and the Osprey.

Falcons and hawks may be smaller but they are just as amazing as their larger cousins. Among them are some of the most specialized birds of prey. They also include many fast and spectacular fliers. And, of course, some are powerful hunters.

▶ *Most birds of prey catch and carry prey with their feet. Before landing at its nest, this Australian Kestrel has transfered the small lizard from its feet to its beak. Compare the shape of the kestrel's wing to the broad wing of the Brahminy Kite opposite. The kestrel is a typical falcon and has a pointed wing.*

Hans & Judy Beste Auscape

primaries

secondaries

cere

upper mandible

lower mandible

breast

primaries

secondaries

tail

tarsus

inner toe

middle toe

outer toe

talons

N.N Birks

▲ *The beautiful Gray Falcon is quite rare. Like many falcons, it has pointed wings, with hard, black flight feathers. It can be a fast and spectacular flier.*

Graceful, gray kites

Mention the word "kite" and most people think of something colorful you fly at the end of a string on windy days. A few people think of brown carrion-eating birds of prey seen around towns in Europe, Asia, and Africa. But there are beautiful white-tailed kites—gray and white birds—that feed on small rodents.

Widespread distribution

The six white-tailed kites are distributed widely around the world. Four of them belong to the genus *Elanus*, which is a group of similar, closely related species.

The same or different?

Three of the *Elanus* kites are so similar that scientists do not agree whether they are local versions of the same species or separate species. At the moment they are usually classed as three species: the White-tailed Kite *Elanus leucurus*, which lives in the southern USA and south-wards to central Argentina; the Black-shouldered Kite *Elanus caeruleus*, in Africa, Spain, and eastwards through Asia to southern China, Indonesia, and New Guinea; and the Black-winged Kite *Elanus notatus*, in Australia. The three species are alike in appearance and behavior, but they differ a little in size, shape, the shade of gray on their upperparts, and the markings on their underwing.

Similar but different

The fourth member of the genus is the Letter-winged Kite *Elanus scriptus*, of Australia. (Australia is the only continent where there are two types of *Elanus*.) The Letter-winged Kite looks rather like the other three kites. It is gray and white, with red eyes outlined by black feathers. Like them, it has a large head, an owl-like face, and pointed wings. But the Letter-winged Kite hunts at night.

Graeme Chapman/Auscape

The cost of making eggs

The eggs of the Black-winged Kite are blotched with purple-brown. Every egg is differently marked. Each egg weighs about 9 per cent of the female's body weight. This means that a clutch of three or more eggs costs her at least 27 per cent of her own weight. She cannot afford to lose this much body weight and so must eat more during the time she is forming eggs. To help her, the male brings food to her.

▲ *The Black-shouldered Kite has a rather owl-like face, and striking ruby-red eyes outlined with black feathers. When perched, its black shoulders, and wingtips that extend below its tail, help to identify it.*

In the air

In flight the Black-shouldered Kite is easy to recognize. Its underparts are white except for dove-gray flight feathers and a black patch in the angle of the wing. Its wings are pointed, and the tail is almost square-tipped. It often hovers while searching for mice.

More sociable than the others, it spends its life in flocks, and its only "territory" is its nest. In contrast, the other kites form flocks in the non-breeding season but separate into lone pairs (a male and a female) to breed; the pairs are highly territorial and aggressively chase away other kites that come into their breeding territory.

Don't compete

One of the "rules" of nature is that when two animal species have identical lifestyles, they cannot live together in the same area. This is because they would have to compete with each other for food, space, nest-sites, and the other things they need to survive and breed.

So that they don't compete with each other, similar species differ in one of several ways: 1. geographic range (where they are found in the world, e.g. North America); 2. habitat (the type of place where they live, e.g. grasslands); 3. feeding location or hunting method; or 4. type of prey eaten.

The four *Elanus* kites not only look alike, but also they live in similar ways. All occur in open country with scattered trees. They are nomads, and they wander to places where food is temporarily easy to get. They hunt from perches or by hovering, and they drop down onto prey with wings held high. The impact

often kills the prey. Otherwise the kite squeezes its victim to death with its talons. More than most birds of prey, kites appear to use their sense of hearing to help locate prey. They often hunt over long grass where prey is not always visible. They all prefer to eat rodents (mice, rats, voles). When rodents are plentiful, the kites may raise two or three broods of chicks in a year.

Three of the *Elanus* kites are found in different parts of the world. That is how they avoid competing. But what happens in Australia, where there are two kinds?

Two Australian kites

Usually, the two Australian kites live in different parts of the country. The Letter-winged Kite is found along some of the inland rivers, which often dry up during droughts. The Black-winged Kite lives in better-watered areas, in open woodland, farmland, and the outskirts of cities. The Black-winged Kite hunts in the daytime, mostly in the early morning and again late in the afternoon, but sometimes after dusk. The Letter-winged Kite is able to hunt in daylight but, especially when breeding, hunts at night, even when there is no moon. So the two species live in different areas and habitats, or hunt at different times. In this way they avoid competing.

▼ *The Letter-winged Kite has an extended band of black running along the underside of its wing.*

◄ *The Letter-winged Kite is found in inland Australia. It is sociable and lives in flocks all year. During the day, as many as 100 kites roost together in trees. By night, they hunt rats.*

All sorts of amazing American kites

A feature that helps a bird to perform a particular function is called an adaptation. An adaptation helps a bird to survive. The shape of its beak, the strength of its feet, and the length of its wings all adapt a bird of prey to its lifestyle, especially to the way it hunts and the types of animals it catches.

Adaptations

The eleven kites of North and South America provide good examples of different adaptation. They have evolved (developed over a long time) into a variety of types. All have the usual hooked beak and curved talons of a bird of prey, but in some kites they have been modified (changed) for a special purpose: some to catch and eat mice; others to pick up snails and extract them from their shells. The way the kites look can be explained by their lifestyle.

The **Snail Kite** has a very long, sharply curved upper beak. It lives mainly on large marsh snails and uses its extraordinary beak to extract the snails from their shells. It has long, broad wings, which help to keep the kite in the air as it flaps slowly about, searching for prey. During the cooler parts of the day, when the snails come to the surface, the kite flies low over the water until it spots a snail. It dives down, grabs the snail in one foot, and flies with it to a perch.

M.P. Kahl/Bruce Coleman Ltd

Deeply forked tail

Stiff and very long outer tail feathers help to make the Swallow-tailed Kite amazingly agile in the air. The graceful bird can rise, fall, float, and dart with ease.

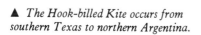

▲ *The Hook-billed Kite occurs from southern Texas to northern Argentina.*

▲ *Freshwater marshes are the habitat of the Snail Kite. This kite is found in Florida and Cuba, and from Mexico to Argentina. It is not common in Florida, but in Argentina there are colonies of as many as a hundred pairs nesting together in bushes or clumps of swamp-grass surrounded by water.*

How does the Snail Kite remove the snail from its shell? It holds the shell in one foot and removes the operculum (a hard cap that plugs the hole when the snail pulls itself into its shell). Then the kite pushes its long upper beak into the shell until it cuts the muscle that holds the snail in, pulls out the juicy body, swallows it, and drops the empty shell. The ground below a kite's favorite perch is often littered with hundreds of empty shells.

Although the Snail Kite sometimes eats other prey, it depends on snails. When marshes are drained, the large snails disappear and so do the kites. This has happened over much of the Everglades, Florida, where the kite was once common. Still, the kite is sometimes called the Everglade Kite.

Unlike the Snail Kite, the **Mississippi Kite** has benefited from human activity. It is adapted to life in open woodlands and now breeds on the Great Plains of North America where people have planted trees. It has long, pointed wings and a very buoyant and acrobatic flight. By day, it spends a lot of time in flight catching flying insects, which it eats on the wing. In fall, when there are very few insects in North America, it migrates in flocks to South America where insects are abundant.

The **Hook-billed Kite** feeds on snails, which it catches in trees and on the ground. It is a secretive bird and usually lives among dense undergrowth. It extracts snails neatly from their shells, but how it does so is not known. It has a very different beak from the Snail Kite, so it may not use the same method to get the snail out of the shell.

The very beautiful **Swallow-tailed Kite** catches prey and eats it in flight. Sometimes it even drinks and bathes on the wing. It flies low over water, wets its belly, and takes a sip of water as it passes. Its main food is flying insects, but it also takes small lizards and the nestlings of small birds. It grabs the whole nest and eats the chicks as it flies along. Its long wings and long tail make it an agile flier.

The small **Pearl Kite**, with pointed wings, is shaped like a falcon. Compared with most kites, it has strong feet and talons. These suit it to a more aggressive hunting method. It catches flying insects but also tackles birds and lizards.

▲ *The graceful Swallow-tailed Kite can be seen from the southern United States (where it is migratory) to Argentina.*

Some names make sense

Elanoides forficatus is the scientific name of the Swallow-tailed Kite. *Elanoides* comes from the Latin language and means "resembling a kite"; *forficatus* means "forked, like scissors". In shape, the kite resembles a large swallow. It has a more deeply forked tail than any other bird of prey. Only the tail of the small Scissor-tailed Kite of Africa (sometimes called the African Swallow-tailed Kite) is nearly as forked.

▲ *The tiny Pearl Kite prefers fairly open country and parkland. It is found in South America, from Nicaragua to northern Argentina.*

13

The gregarious Black Kite

Black Kites are found in warmer parts of the world, except the Americas. They are often the most common and obvious birds of prey. Black Kites are also among the most gregarious (sociable) of all birds of prey. They roost, bathe, sun themselves, feed, and move around in large flocks or small groups.

Hundreds of Black Kites scavenge in some towns and villages. In New Delhi, India, 2400 pairs were counted—a density of 41 pairs per square mile. There they are tolerated by humans, while feeding on garbage and animal carcasses. In Australia, flocks gather at slaughterhouses to wait for offal.

In the breeding season the kites split into lone pairs (a male and a female). Sometimes, when there is a lot of food and not many nest-sites, they breed close together. At one oasis 30 pairs nested, with nests about 125 meters (400 feet) apart.

Jozef Mihok/Survival Anglia

Black Kites and fire

Attracted by the smoke of grass fires, Black Kites gather from far and wide. Flocks of them fly to and fro ahead of the spreading fire and catch animals fleeing the flames. Afterwards, they pick up burnt or smoke-dazed animals among the ashes. The Australian Aborigines believed that the kite spread fire intentionally, so that it got more food. A few Aboriginal tribes used fire to bring kites in close enough to a hidden person to be caught. They ate the kites and used their feathers in belts and as decorations in ceremonies.

◄ *Occasionally Black Kites nest in groups, but usually they nest as lone pairs. This is an unusually large brood. (Generally the kites have two chicks.) Notice the blue and red plastic and string that the parents have used to line the nest. These kites often bring such items to their nest, including garments snatched from clothes lines.*

▲ *Before dark, Black Kites gather and circle in a flock, then settle for the night. They often have a favorite roost tree, which they may use every winter for years. As many as 500 Black Kites, sometimes with a few Red Kites, may share a roost. In the morning they scatter to search for food as far as 48 kilometers (30 miles) away.*

▶ *At five weeks old, these chicks are already the same size as their parents. They can defend themselves against many predators but do not have much luck scaring the photographer away. They will fledge (make their first flight) in another week or so.*

Fishing with bait?

Black Kites are clever hunters. One picked up some bread left by picnickers and dropped it into a river. It then flew to a perch overhanging the water and watched. When fish came up to nibble at the bread the kite swooped down and, after several attempts, caught one. Later it put more bread out. It seemed to be using the bread as bait to attract fish.
How did it learn this trick?

▲ *Like the sea eagles, Black Kites sometimes scoop live fish from water.*

Soaring scavengers of seashore and swamp

Typical kites are medium-sized birds of prey that soar often and feed on dead animals and other scraps. Two of them, the Brahminy Kite and the Whistling Kite, prefer to live in wet habitats.

Distribution—where in the world?

The Brahminy Kite is found in the tropics, from India to southern China, down through the islands of South-east Asia, to New Guinea, the Solomon Islands, and the north coast of Australia. The distribution of the Whistling Kite extends upwards from Australia to New Guinea and New Caledonia. The two distributions meet and overlap in northern Australia and New Guinea, so that both kites are found in these regions.

Habitat—where in particular?

Perhaps the simplest definition of habitat is "the kind of place where an animal prefers to live". A habitat is a particular type of environment such as a forest, a swamp, or a desert. Many birds of prey are found in several habitats. Sometimes they live there all year; sometimes they move from one habitat to another at different seasons. The important point about any habitat is that it must provide the bird with a suitable food supply and, in the breeding season, with a nest-site.

Hans & Judy Beste/Auscape

▲ *Whistling Kites gather on a dead wallaby. They have quite strong beaks and can eat large animals, but they are not capable of killing them.*

◄ *The Brahminy Kite is a medium-sized bird of prey. In the Northern Hemisphere a typical Brahminy Kite has darkish shafts to its white feathers. This gives it a streaked appearance. Farther south, the kite has a pure white head and breast.*

Several birds of prey live in aquatic habitats—that is, near water. The Brahminy Kite and the Whistling Kite occur around lakes, rivers, swamps, marshes, sea coasts, and estuaries. The Brahminy Kite is largely coastal, especially in Australia. In countries further north it is also found in forest clearings, gardens, and rice paddies. In highlands it soars above rainforest. In parts of Asia it is very tame and often lives near humans.

The Whistling Kite extends into drier areas than the Brahminy Kite. It is found well inland, along rivers. It even lives in the dry center of Australia, usually around waterholes, but sometimes far into the desert. Occasionally

it joins flocks of Black Kites around carrion or slaughterhouses. Like the Brahminy Kite it lives in seaside towns and feeds on fishermen's scraps. In its choice of habitat it is in between the wet-country Brahminy Kite and the dry-country Black Kite. Perhaps it could be called a moist-country kite!

Scavengers and thieves
The Brahminy Kite has the rather weak beak and feet of a raptor that lives on small, harmless prey and food scraps. The Whistling Kite is also a great scavenger and has similar feeding habits. But it can catch small rabbits, starlings, waterbirds, and other live prey. It has a more powerful beak and feet than the Brahminy Kite, so it is suited to a more predatory way of hunting. Bold and aggressive, the Whistling Kite often steals prey from ibis, herons, other kites, and even sea eagles. In an effort to make an eagle drop its prey, the kite will swoop at the larger bird over and over again. The agile kite can easily avoid the large eagle if the eagle strikes out. Occasionally, the cheeky kite even darts down to snatch food from the eagle's beak.

▼ *Head thrown back, a Whistling Kite calls to advertise its territory ownership. It whistles often: a long descending "seeo" followed by a high, sharp "si si si si", which carries long distances. The call is instantly recognizable.*

A soaring kite shape
The beautiful chestnut and white plumage of the Brahminy Kite is unmistakable. The young birds, in their browner plumage, could be mistaken for Whistling Kites, but their underwing pattern is different and their tail shorter.

Brahminy Kite: handsome scrounger

Like all the soaring kites, the Brahminy Kite has long, broad, "fingered" wings. Such wings enable the kite to soar and glide, wheel and bank with ease. The outer wing feathers (the primaries) form "fingers". They are thought to help reduce turbulence (rough air currents) at the wingtip—useful to prevent stalling when the kite flies slowly. They also give the kite extra lift so that it can stay in the air with little effort.

The kite circles widely in the air, usually just above the treetops, searching below for food. When it spots something tasty it either sweeps down in a wide circle or spirals tightly down. It swoops down to snatch food from the ground, from trees, or water, seldom getting wet. It eats small items in flight but carries larger prey to a perch, in a tree or on the mast of a ship, before tearing it up.

The Brahminy Kite occasionally catches live fish, up to 450 grams (1 pound), about half the kite's weight, from just below the water's surface. It expertly snatches scraps washed up along the shore ; floating bits and pieces from the water; insects from the foliage of trees; small animals on the road killed by cars; crabs; mice; small snakes; sick birds; and frogs. It also steals food from other birds. The kite is not a powerful hunter, nor is it choosy about its diet. One author described it as the most regal of all scavengers. He wondered how so handsome a bird could have such unpleasant habits.

▲ *Its wings held high and sharply bent, this Brahminy Kite strains to lift its large catch clear of the water. More usually, these kites snatch small bits of food from the water's surface, or scrounge for dead animals along the shore.*

▶ *Young Brahminy Kites are brown. They go through a complete molt once a year and take several years to change, gradually, into the handsome red and white of an adult.*

▲ *The warm waters preferred by the Brahminy Kite support an abundance of animal life in and around the water, so the kite has plenty to eat.*

Kites kept London clean

It is hard to believe that as long ago as 1560, in London, England, Red Kites were protected. The kites were very common in the city. Often they would swoop down to pick up scraps in the marketplace, and even snatch food from children. They caught rats and insects, disposed of animal bodies, and ate various kinds of human waste. They were valued because they helped to keep the city clean at a time when there were no good garbage-disposal systems. Today, Red Kites are rare in Britain; the cities are too clean.

Colorful males, many mates

There are thirteen species of harriers, widely distributed around the world in open areas. All are very similar and easily recognized as a harrier. The males of some species are strikingly colored and may have several mates. The plainer males of the other harriers have one mate only (as do most birds of prey).

Harrier habits

Harriers have long, narrow wings, often held in a shallow V-shape. They flap low and slow across grassland, marsh, and moor. Carefully they fly to and fro, checking an area for prey: small mammals and birds, reptiles and insects. The harriers that prefer marshlands eat frogs and fish—it depends on what is available locally. They also eat carrion—either the unfinished prey of another predator, or animals that have died, including road-traffic victims.

Harriers prefer open country: some occur in marshes, others in dry grasslands. With one exception, they have little use for trees. The Spotted Harrier roosts and nests in trees. Sometimes, however, it roosts on the ground, as do all the other harriers. The other harriers also nest on the ground.

Share the work

The breeding "chores" are divided between the harrier pair. The male hunts for the family, during courtship and then until several weeks after the young begin to fly. The female incubates and protects the eggs and chicks, but usually does not help with the hunting until the chicks are about three weeks old.

As he returns with food, the male calls the female off the nest. She flies up to meet him, rolls on her back, and extends her legs to catch the prey he drops to her. She then returns to the nest and pulls off small pieces of flesh, which she offers to the chicks.

Sexual dimorphism

Sexual dimorphism means a difference in form between males and females. In this case, the sexes differ in size and weight: female harriers are about one and a half times as heavy as their males. In the Northern Harrier, which is also called the Hen Harrier in England and the Marsh Hawk in America, females weigh about 525 grams (18½ ounces) and males 350 grams (12½ ounces).

Grounded

Most harriers build their nest among tall grass, reeds, or shrubs. They lay a large clutch. Northern Harriers can have as many as seven eggs, but five is usual. Because they nest on the ground, their eggs and chicks are at risk from predatory mammals such as foxes and cats. The only tree-nesting harrier, the Spotted Harrier, lays three eggs.

▲ *The African Marsh Harrier roosts and breeds in marshes and reedbeds south of the Sahara Desert, but also hunts over grassland.*

Sexual dichromatism

Sexual dichromatism means that the male and female differ in color. This is unusual in birds of prey, for in most species the sexes are of similar coloration. In some harriers (but not all of them) the male is more brightly colored than the female. For example, males of the Northern Harrier and Montagu's Harrier are silver-gray, and those of the African Marsh Harrier are black. All the females, as well as the young birds of both sexes, are brown. So different are they in color and size that, in the past, people thought the males and females belonged to two different species.

Why is the adult male more colorful than the female? To breed, the male must attract a mate. His color signals that he is a mature male. Maybe females find the brighter males more attractive.

One mate or many?

Most birds of prey are monogamous. They stay with one partner for the whole of the breeding season and may stay with the same partner year after year. However, some of the harriers are polygynous—that is, one male has several mates at the same time. Occasionally, in the Northern Harrier, up to six females share one male. He feeds them all during courtship, but his first mate lays first and her eggs hatch first. He spends more time helping her feed the chicks than he does with the other mates. As a result his other mates are not able to raise many young. They must look after the brood and hunt to feed them.

When rodents (mice, voles) are plentiful, more Northern Harriers are polygynous. In a season when rodents are scarce, few harriers can afford more than one mate. The number of mates a male has seems to depend, at least in part, on how many females he can keep well fed during courtship.

Left-footed

Raptors and parrots use their feet to hold food or to catch prey. Most seem to be left-footed. One study showed that Black-shouldered Kites catch prey with their left foot twice as often as with their right. When they use both feet, they strike first, or in the most vulnerable part (the upper body), with their left foot.

▲ *The beautiful Spotted Harrier of Australia shows all the features of a typical harrier: long wings, long tail, and long legs. Its owlish face, framed by a ridge of short stiff feathers, is also characteristic. There is some disagreement about the function of the ridge. It may collect sound and funnel it to the harrier's extra-large ear openings. This would help the harrier to find animals out of sight, moving through the grass.*

▶ *A Montagu's Harrier drops on a vole as it crosses an open patch of ground. The harrier doesn't need bare ground to hunt successfully. By listening for their rustles and squeaks, it can find animals hidden in the grass, and its long legs can reach deep into tall grass.*

Hellio & Van Ingen/NHPA

21

Out of Africa

There is a great variety of raptors in Africa. Identifying them can be difficult. The harrier hawks and chanting goshawks are long-legged raptors, colored gray as adults, but brown in their first year or two. Each has an unusual way of hunting, and they are very different in appearance and habits.

Many African raptors

There are about 90 species of raptors in Africa. Some live there year-round; others are regular visitors, which return to Europe to breed. The harrier hawks and chanting goshawks are found only in the African region.

▶ *The strange-looking African Harrier Hawk.*

Harriers or hawks?

The two harrier hawks—one in Africa and the other in Madagascar—live in open woodland, farmland, or grassland with trees. Strange-looking birds, they have a small head and a bare face. In some ways they are like harriers, but in other ways they are more like goshawks.

The African Harrier Hawk has a long tail, long flexible wings, and a large wing area for its weight. These make it very buoyant in the air. Usually it flies low and slow over or through the tree canopy. Occasionally it jinks to the side to grab an insect or land on a perch.

What bird is it?

Occasionally the African Harrier Hawk soars. Then its small slim head, very large wing area (long and broad), and distinctive broad white band across the middle of its tail can be seen.

Q. Why do harrier hawks blush?

A. Harrier hawks have featherless faces. The skin is gray in the hawk's first year, and it brightens to the yellow of an adult by three years of age. When the hawk is excited—during mating, and when threatening another bird—its yellow face blushes pink.

▼ *A harrier hawk perches quietly in a tree. Because it does not attract attention to itself, it can easily be overlooked.*

Stephen Dalton/NHPA

Mainly it eats insects, lizards, nestling birds, roosting bats, and squirrels, but will also eat oil-palm fruit.

Where no other can reach

The harrier hawk is double-jointed. It has long legs that it can bend backwards or forwards, through an angle of 70 degrees from the vertical. It can also bend them out to the side through 30 degrees each way. Such a flexible leg joint allows the harrier hawk to reach deep into holes in cliffs or trees. It stretches in and grabs roosting bats or nestling birds.

The harrier hawk snatches with one leg, while it hangs from the entrance to the hole with the other leg. Only one other raptor, the Crane Hawk of South America, has double-jointed legs and can hunt in this way. Both harrier hawks also have a small, slim head, enabling them to peer into small holes and under pieces of bark. Because no other raptor hunts in this way, these hawks have no competition from other raptors.

Thorough searcher

Someone studied the African Harrier Hawk hunting. It flew from tree to tree and visited an average of 31 trees in an hour. At one tree it might spend 30 minutes or more, making a careful search, peering under the bark and into holes. On average, it found prey in six of the 31 trees searched each hour.

Tricky nest robber

The harrier hawk often hangs upside down, wings flapping, from a clump of weaverbird nests. It forces its head inside one nest after another and removes the nestlings.

As the hawk flies through the trees, starlings and other small birds mob it (try to drive it away). It flies back and forth until the birds, in their panic, reveal the location of their nests. Then it steals their eggs or nestlings.

Chanting goshawks

Chanting goshawks are often quite common. Ten or more can be seen in a day in Somalia or Namibia. They often perch in the open on telegraph poles, tree stumps, or termite mounds. Even during the hottest part of the day, when most other hawks are resting in the shade, chanting goshawks are active.

When hunting they fly from perch to perch, searching the surrounding area. Often they catch lizards and insects, mostly by flying down from a perch, but also by walking about on the ground. Sometimes they stamp around rodent burrows to try to get rats to come out. They can be powerful hunters and occasionally catch a bird in flight or take a guinea fowl three times their own weight.

▼ The Pale Chanting Goshawk is one of three types of chanting goshawk. The others are the Eastern Chanting Goshawk and the Dark Chanting Goshawk. They all occur in Africa and are very alike in appearance and habits.

Peter Steyn/Ardea London

Tuneful chanters

A pale inner wing, which contrasts with a dark outer wing, separates the chanting goshawks from other goshawks. Their black and white barred tail is also distinctive. In other ways too, the chanting goshawks are a little different from the true goshawks in the next chapter. They belong to the genus *Melierax*, which means "a singing hawk". This refers to their tuneful whistling call. At the beginning of the breeding season, they perch in the top of a tree, or fly about, and call again and again. Although they do not sing like a songbird, they make quite a pleasant sound. The chant probably advertises the territory ownership of a pair, or if the bird is single, the chant may attract a mate.

▲ With long legs and short toes, the Eastern Chanting Goshawk walks and runs with ease. Many other raptors are clumsy on the ground. This goshawk is found in drier parts of eastern Africa and is often seen on the ground.

Agile accipiters

Accipiters are found in woodlands all around the world. Most are small to medium-sized bird-catchers. They are aggressive agile hunters, which make good use of surprise in their attack.

Explain a name

Accipiters are the goshawks and sparrowhawks. The strange name comes from the Latin word *accipiter*, which means simply "a hawk". The "sparrow-" and the "gos-" of their common names refer to the prey they catch: sparrows for the smaller hawks, and geese for the larger (although they rarely catch and eat geese).

About accipiters

The genus *Accipiter* contains about 48 species. Found all around the world, accipiters live in many types of woodland: from pine forest to lush rainforest and dry thornbush. They have broad, often short wings, long tails and longish legs. Their beak is short, but sharp.

The largest of all accipiters is the Northern Goshawk of North America, Europe, and Asia, which weighs up to 2 kilograms (almost 4½ pounds) and is 48–61 centimeters (19–24 inches) long. It preys on mammals such as hares and rabbits, and birds such as crows and grouse. The smallest is the Little Sparrowhawk of Africa, weighing up to about 105 grams (3¾ ounces), the size of a thrush. It eats small birds and flying insects snatched from the air.

In between, there are all sizes of hawk. Most eat mainly birds, but also small mammals and reptiles. All accipiters are bold hunters that catch their prey using stealth and agility. They can twist and turn with ease as they dash through a thicket in pursuit of prey.

▼ *Accipiters split parental duties. When the chicks are young, the male hunts for the family. The female broods the chicks, tears the prey up, and gently offers small pieces to them. They reach up and take the food from her beak.*

Clem Haagner/Ardea London

David A. Ponton

▲ *Northern Goshawks are large, powerful hawks that live on hares and large birds. They nest in woodland and forest in Europe, Asia, and North America. Pairs nest in the same area each year—not always in the same tree, but nearby. Some females will attack savagely if you go too close to their nest.*

▶ *During breeding the male sparrowhawk gives food to his female in a spectacular aerial pass.*

Big females

In nearly all raptors the female is larger than the male. This is the opposite to most of the animals around us, in which the males are larger, such as dogs, chickens (roosters), cattle (bulls), and people.

The accipiters are among the most dimorphic of all raptors. That is, they have a large difference in size between the sexes. This is connected with their diet. Bird-catchers are most dimorphic, next come mammal-catchers, and carrion-eaters are the least dimorphic (little difference in size between males and females).

Feeding when breeding

In the dimorphic species, including accipiters, there is a split of parental duties during breeding. The male does all the hunting, for himself and his family, until the chicks are about half-grown. The female does most of the incubation of the eggs. She broods the chicks and shares out the food the male has brought in. As the male flies in with a catch, he calls. She flies out to meet him and takes the prey from his feet. Alternatively, he may give the prey to her at a favorite perch. During courtship, he also feeds her and performs flying displays, presumably to show her that he is a good flier and hunter.

David A. Ponton

Large and small

The female Cooper's Hawk on the left weighs about 560 grams (19 ounces), the male on the right only 380 grams (13 ounces). The female can catch larger prey than the male can.

▶ *Because they tend to stay among trees, accipiters can live almost unnoticed around cities. The Brown Goshawk lives in Canberra, Australia's capital city. Only in the breeding season, when it displays high above the trees, is it really obvious. But the worried twittering of small birds sometimes gives it away as it passes through a garden.*

P. & J. Olsen

Functional feathers

The plumage (all the feathers) of a bird must be kept in top condition. It helps to keep the bird warm on cold days and cool on hot days. It keeps the hawk dryish (but not totally waterproof) and, of course, airworthy (able to fly).

Identifying species and ages

Feathers also serve another function. They are social signals whose color reveals age, sex, and species. In some accipiter species, the males are slightly different in color to the females. In most accipiters, the plumage in the first year of life is different from that in later years; the breast is streaked in the juveniles and barred in the adults. So different are the males and females, young birds and adults of some species that nineteenth-century bird-watchers thought they were different species altogether.

An odd pair

Normally, different species do not breed together. But for several years a female Brown Goshawk has produced hybrid chicks, fathered by a Variable Goshawk (white form). They live in a typical habitat for Variable Goshawks, but around them the land has been cleared so that only patches of woodland remain. No female Variable Goshawks have been seen in the area, so the male may have been forced to accept an odd partner.

Such a cross happens occasionally, where similar species occur together, and one or both are uncommon. Black Kites and Red Kites breed together in parts of Europe where both species are rare. Obviously, their behavior (which does differ slightly) must be similar

Fussy with feathers

If you have ever found and handled a feather, you will have quickly discovered how easy it is to mess up its neat arrangement, and how difficult it is to straighten again. Yet raptors and other birds seem to keep their feathers tidy with little trouble. During the day, a bird grooms often. It rubs its head on its body and scratches it with one foot. It runs its beak through the body and flight feathers, to straighten them and to spread oil, which it nibbles from an oil gland at the base of the tail. The oil stops the feathers getting dry and waterproofs them. It may also have some anti-fungal and anti-bacterial properties to prevent infections.

With time, the feathers gradually become worn and tatty, so they are replaced periodically during a molt. Most raptors replace all their feathers every year, but some large species keep their feathers for two or more years.

Raptors also bathe: some wade into water to wash, others have a dust bath. A few fly through dew or raindrops hanging from leaves. Some also lie on the ground and let ants crawl through their feathers. The ants give off formic acid which may help to keep parasites out of the feathers.

▼ In a patch of Australian woodland, two species—a female Brown Goshawk and a male Variable Goshawk—paired and have produced chicks for several years. The odd combination is like a lion mating with a leopard, or a zebra with a horse.

▲ *Long, thin legs and toes make the Collared Sparrowhawk a successful hunter of small birds in the air.*

▼ *The Black-mantled Goshawk's orange eye is a sign of maturity.*

enough to be acceptable to each other. In most kinds of animals, hybrids between different species are infertile and cannot produce young themselves. This is true for some raptors too— as we know from hybrids in captivity.

Masters of surprise

Accipiters most often search for prey by perch-hunting: looking and listening. They glide from tree to tree, usually perching among the leaves, out of sight. Occasionally they still-hunt, by waiting motionless until prey comes within striking distance. When prey is spotted they chase, helter-skelter through the trees.

A study of Northern Goshawks showed that if a goshawk caught a pigeon after a short chase, it was often a fat healthy pigeon. If the pigeon was caught after a long chase, then it was usually weak and thin. This is because goshawks cannot outfly a healthy bird, only

a sick one, but they can catch a healthy bird by surprise.

A typical accipiter hunting technique is for the hawk to fly low along one side of a hedge or bank, then flip up and over and onto a flock of unsuspecting small birds on the other side. It seizes one as they take flight.

The long legs and slender toes of many accipiters, especially the sparrowhawks, are ideal for catching agile birds in the air. They must be able to capture the bird, but the impact is not great. The larger goshawks have thicker legs and toes, and can hit prey on the ground with great force.

Several types together

Sometimes there are several types of accipiters living in the same area. Papua New Guinea probably has the greatest number: three, four, or five are found on each of various islands in the region. There, some are strikingly colored: combinations of black, brown, white, and rich rufous (red). Little is known about any of them.

In North America there are three accipiters: the large Northern Goshawk, the medium-sized Cooper's Hawk, and the small Sharp-shinned Hawk. Because males and females are very different in size, that makes six size classes of accipiter. They avoid competing with each other by taking different types of prey and different-sized prey, or by hunting in a slightly different manner or habitat.

In much of Europe there are only two accipiters. The Northern Goshawk catches prey up to 4 kilograms (8¾ pounds; an adult hare). The small Eurasian Sparrowhawk catches birds up the size of a woodpigeon, about half a kilogram (1 pound).

Look into their eyes

Did you know that you can tell what age some accipiters are by looking into their eyes? The color of their eyes changes with age—from brown in their first year to a deep yellow, orange, or wine-red over the next year or two. When their eyes are fully colored, they are adult. The hawks have color vision. The color in their eye may filter out certain shades, so that they can pick out prey from its surroundings more easily.

▲ *Short wings and a long tail allow the Eurasian Sparrowhawk to make short dashes between trees and shrubs after small birds.*

Dying young; living long

Many raptors die young. Those that reach adulthood often live long lives. By studying raptor deaths it is often possible to prevent unnecessary losses.

Tough early years

More than half of all raptor chicks die in their first year of life partly through their inexperience. To us, it seems sad, but it is part of the balance of nature. Many young birds must die, otherwise there would be too many birds for the habitat to support. All that is needed is enough birds of breeding age to replace the adults that die.

How do they die?

Once the chicks are flying and have left their parents, life can be tough. The young hawks are inexperienced hunters. They spend their first year or so wandering, without a territory, and must find prey and hunt in places they don't know. Older hawks may chase them away. Many starve.

Bad weather—a severe storm, for example— may kill raptors outright. Or it may prevent them hunting. Sometimes birds of prey are themselves preyed upon! Occasionally larger raptors eat smaller raptors. Some big owls catch quite a few daytime raptors.

Many raptors die because of humans. They are hit by cars, shot, electrocuted, and poisoned. They fly into windows or high wires. They die because we destroy their homes and they have nowhere else to go. Fortunately, some of these deaths can be prevented.

Understanding raptors helps to prevent unnecessary deaths. That's why it is important to try to answer questions such as: What causes raptors to die? How old are they when they die? Which birds die and why?

If too many raptors are dying, and we can find out why, it is often possible to do something about it. Organochlorine pesticides were banned in many countries when scientists showed that they were killing birds or causing them to lay eggs with shells so thin that they cracked under the parents. Because of studies of electrocuted raptors, new electricity lines are often built so that they are raptor-safe.

The flip side to death is survival. Only the toughest survive to breed, so that the raptor population stays strong and healthy.

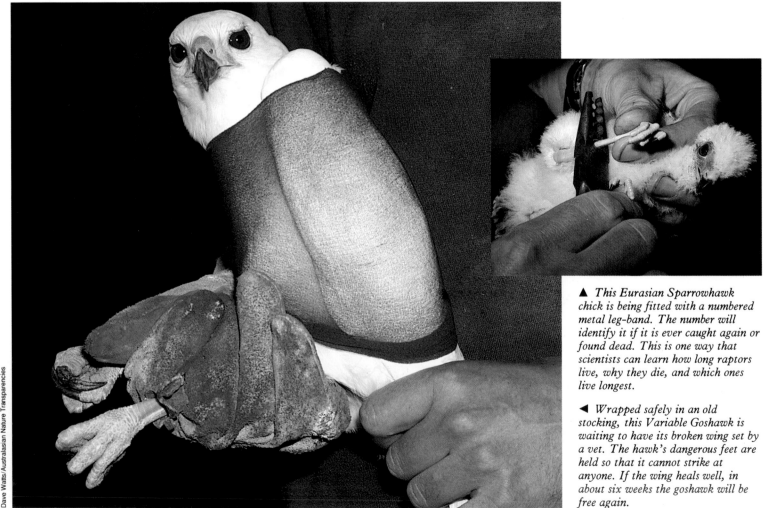

▲ *This Eurasian Sparrowhawk chick is being fitted with a numbered metal leg-band. The number will identify it if it is ever caught again or found dead. This is one way that scientists can learn how long raptors live, why they die, and which ones live longest.*

◄ *Wrapped safely in an old stocking, this Variable Goshawk is waiting to have its broken wing set by a vet. The hawk's dangerous feet are held so that it cannot strike at anyone. If the wing heals well, in about six weeks the goshawk will be free again.*

Dave Watts/Australasian Nature Transparencies

Gordon Langsbury/Bruce Coleman Ltd

Long-lived survivors

Once birds of prey reach adulthood their chances of survival are much better. In fact, some birds of prey can have long lives. The oldest known wild European Kestrel was 16 years of age, and a Honey Buzzard lived until it was nearly 29. Of course, most do not live that long. Like other birds, smaller raptors tend not to live as long as larger raptors. In zoos some eagles have reached more than 50 years of age.

▼ *During the 1960s and 1970s certain pesticides killed countless birds of prey and caused widespread breeding failure. So bad was their effect that some species of raptor disappeared from vast areas of the world. Now many countries ban these pesticides; safer chemicals are available, and their use is better controlled. Birds of prey are returning to some of the deserted areas.*

Davic E. Rowley/Planet Earth Pictures

Terribly tangled

Fast-flying raptors collide easily with wires, nets, and discarded fishing lines. Some die from the impact, others die slowly when broken feathers or a wing stop them from hunting. This one was lucky. It was trapped by a bird-bander and will soon be set free.

What do you do if you find a bird?

If you find a sick or injured bird of prey, remember that its feet and talons are its most lethal weapons. Also keep in mind that if you cover its head it will become quite calm. That is why falconers put hoods on their birds. Pick the bird up with your hands around both legs and both wings, just below where the legs are joined to the body.

As soon as possible, put the bird in a cardboard box. This will keep it calm and prevent it from injuring itself further. It will not do the bird any good if you keep looking in the box and frightening it. Take it to your nearest vet or wildlife rescue group. Or phone someone who knows about birds to get advice.

If the bird has a ring on its leg, make sure you report the number to the address written on the ring. You will then receive information on when and where the bird was ringed, and your report will help scientists to understand more about these birds.

Many people who find chicks on the ground think that they are orphaned, and take them home and feed them. This is the worst thing to do. When the cute baby grows into a huge eagle that won't fly away, and eats the neighbor's cat, they wonder what to do!

In most cases a careful look around will help you find the nest. If the chick is uninjured and big enough to perch, you need only place it on a high branch where cats and dogs can't reach. It will call when it is hungry, and the parents will find it easily.

Tim Shepherd/Oxford Scientific Films

Buzzards

The "buzzards" that circle overhead whenever there is trouble in cowboy movies are, in fact, usually Turkey Vultures. Real buzzards are more attractive hawks that belong to the genus *Buteo*.

Soaring hawks

There are 25 *Buteo* species and several closely related species, including *Parabuteo*. They are found everywhere except India and southwards to Australia. Buzzards are medium-sized soaring hawks, with long, broad wings. Their beak and toes are of medium strength—neither as weak as a kite's nor as strong as an eagle's.

Rough legs and lemmings

The Rough-legged Hawk gets its name from its legs, which are feathered to the top of the feet. (Most other buzzards have bare legs.) Usually it hunts from a prominent perch, swooping down to catch prey on the ground. Even though it takes many other kinds of prey, it is very dependent on small mammals when breeding. In years when there are many lemmings the Rough-legs lay five or six eggs, compared with three or four eggs in an average year.

Eurasian Buzzards also adjust their clutch size, and the number of young they raise, according to the food supply. The Eurasian Buzzard doesn't breed in regions north of the treeline, which is about latitude 65°N. There, in open Arctic and subarctic regions, the similar Rough-legged Hawk replaces it. Both are very variable in color: individuals may be pale or dark, or any shade between. At the other extreme are the Harris' Hawks, which are all identical.

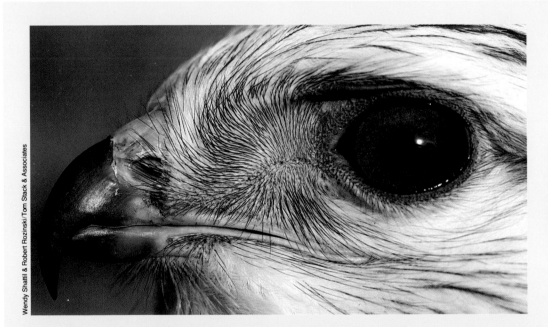

▲ *The Rough-legged Hawk (above and at left) uses a prominent perch to scan for prey. For breeding it likes the open country of subarctic and Arctic North America, Scandinavia, and the far north of Russia.*

Wendy Shattil & Robert Rozinski/Tom Stack & Associates

Are two eyes better than one?

Many birds have largely monocular vision—that is, their eyes are in the sides of their head, and their view of the world is largely through one eye at a time. Birds of prey have monocular vision, but because their eyes are placed in the front of their head, they also see quite a lot of their world through two eyes. The area seen by each eye overlaps in the front of the bird (much as it does in humans). This binocular vision allows birds of prey (and humans) very accurate judgement of depth and distance. To see the difference, try the pencil trick. Hold two pencils, one in each hand, far out from your eyes and try to touch the two points together. Try first with both eyes and then with one eye closed. With one eye closed you have monocular vision, and you'll find it harder to line up the pencils.

A group of Harris' Hawks sees a jackrabbit and flies down to get it.

One hawk flushes the rabbit into the open.

Other hawks ambush the rabbit when it is flushed out.

Co-operation

Harris' Hawks often hunt in groups of four to six. When the Hawks spot a jackrabbit under cover, the group flies over. One or more hawks flush the rabbit into the open, where the others wait in ambush. Co-operation allows the hawks to catch large, dangerous prey (a jackrabbit weighs about twice as much as a female hawk, and three times as much as a male hawk). It also increases their hunting success. The group members share the kill.

Hunting parties

Harris' Hawks do not fit the typical image of the raptor as a lone hunter. They breed in small groups, they hunt in teams, and they share prey. The hunting parties are usually family groups: an adult male and female, and perhaps four of their offspring up to three years of age. On a typical hunt, they break into two's and three's and begin searching, always keeping an eye on the other group members.

When prey (e.g. a jackrabbit) is sighted, they all gather and work together. Sometimes, one after the other, they swoop at the rabbit until it is exhausted. By surprising, confusing, or tiring their large prey, they can overcome it more easily, and with less risk of injury to themselves, than if they were hunting alone. The prey is large enough to provide all the group members with a meal.

Team work helps survival and breeding

In the deserts of New Mexico the larger hunting groups are the most successful; each bird in a large group gets a greater amount of food than does each bird in a small group. Groups also breed more successfully than lone pairs; they are able to raise two broods a year rather than one.

Team hunting works for the Harris' Hawk, so it has become a way of life. Why don't all hawks hunt in teams? Because it is suited to the desert habitat of the Harris' Hawk, where prey is not common and is often large.

► *Typically, the Eurasian Buzzard hunts alone. It is very adaptable and catches a variety of prey, particularly small hares and rabbits, and voles. Found from England, across Europe and Asia to Japan, it eats whatever is suitable and plentiful where it is living. Its diet also changes with the seasons: more rodents in winter; more insects, lizards, caterpillars, even earthworms, in summer.*

Michael Leach/NHPA

Studying raptors

Studying raptors is challenging and essential. Large size and strong flight make them easy to see but hard to approach. We must have a good knowledge of their behavior and needs before sensible decisions can be made to protect them. Besides, they are fascinating birds.

Much to learn

Because many hawks nest in the same area year after year, and their nests are fairly obvious, quite a lot is known about their nesting habits. It is much harder to study them when they aren't breeding. Yet there are many species about which almost nothing is known, because they are rare, hard to find, or live in parts of the world where humans seldom go. Sometimes, common species are ignored, while rarer species, with more urgent problems, are studied. There is still a lot to learn.

To learn how to study raptors, the best place to begin is with a local biologist, science teacher, or bird club. The more you watch the birds, the more patterns you will notice in their behavior. Then you can start to think about why they have those behaviors.

▼ *A biologist checks the nest of a Red-tailed Hawk built on a bluff at the Snake River Birds of Prey Area, in Idaho. The adults slip away before the climber reaches the nest, and they do not attack. Climbing to nests is often dangerous, but it is exciting. It is one way to get close to raptors and learn about them.*

Studying diet

If you find a raptor at a roost or nest, sometimes it is possible to find pellets or remains of prey on the ground below. Pellets are oval-shaped wads of feathers, bones, fur, and other indigestible bits of the prey, brought up (regurgitated) by the hawks. When inspecting the pellets you can often identify what the hawk has eaten. It is useful to know what the hawk eats in all seasons.

Disturbing study

It is always best to be cautious around the nest of a hawk. Some species are likely to desert their eggs and chicks (leave and never return).

A study of the effect of disturbance on Ferruginous Hawks in North America showed that a brief visit by a human 120 meters (130 yards) from the nest caused the parent to flush (leave the nest) 40 per cent of the time. A visit to 250 meters (272 yards) reduced flushing to 10 per cent. Disturbance caused the desertion of one-third of the nests visited, and fewer young were raised compared with undisturbed nests. The moral of this story is that, unless you have a good reason to visit a nest, it is best to keep away. But not all raptor species are as sensitive as the Ferruginous Hawk.

▼ *Ferruginous Hawk are shy birds. They breed on cliffs or in trees on undisturbed plains and high deserts.*

They have an unusually wide gape. Some biologists think that this may help the hawks to keep cool when panting. Keeping cool is particularly important for the chicks, many of which, like these three, are in the hot sun all day.

S. Krasemann/NHPA

Protected at Snake River

Snake River Birds of Prey Area, Idaho, is maintained by the United States government. An area of 247 000 hectares (610 000 acres) along the Snake River is set aside for about 700 pairs of birds, of 15 different species. Here biologists check a Ferruginous Hawk nest.

W. Perry Conway/Tom Stack & Associates

Flying south for the winter

Each year millions of birds fly from one part of the world to the other. In fall, they leave their breeding grounds and migrate hundreds or even thousands of miles. The journey can be exhausting and dangerous. Come spring, they make the return trip.

Mysterious migration

Humans have been watching and wondering at the mysterious movements of birds for centuries. Even today some people use the seasonal arrival of migrating hawks as a signal that it is time to plant their crops. We are still learning about migration and discovering new routes (new to us, but not to the birds!).

Migration is a regular movement between breeding areas and non-breeding areas. It is a feature of many birds of prey that live at higher latitudes and higher altitudes, where it gets very cold in winter. Migration brings the birds to places where the conditions are best for that time of year.

From some places, all the raptors leave for the winter (full migration); from others, only some leave (partial migration). In a winter with lots of prey, more may stay than in a winter when prey are scarce. Usually the adult males are more likely to remain than the adult females and youngsters. Other raptors make movements that aren't as regular or predictable as migration; they wander to where food is temporarily plentiful.

Which way?

The most obvious migrations are north–south. Raptors that breed at high latitudes across

Migration hard to study

Each year, Broad-winged Hawks join the flow of raptors passing through Panama. For several years, a biologist studying the migration photographed the raptors as they soared over. He projected the photos onto a screen and counted every single dot. In October–November one year he counted 2.5 million birds of prey. Later he discovered that many more were passing over too high to be seen, some possibly as high as 7000 meters (23 000 feet).

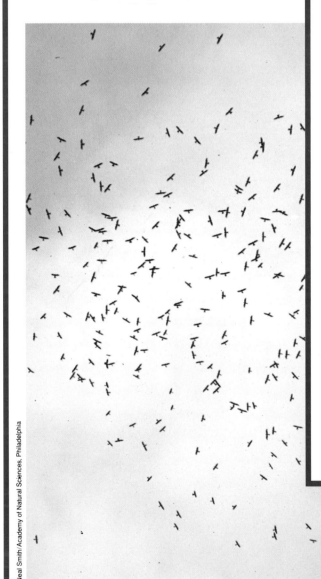

◀ *This sky full of raptors is just a tiny part of a steady flow of Broad-winged Hawks that passes through Panama each October–November. The hawks circle effortlessly in thermals.*

Europe and Asia move towards the equator, either to Africa or South-east Asia. From North America they move to South America. The pattern is less obvious in Australia. There the raptors that do migrate move north, rather than south, in the winter. They avoid the wet seasons as well as cold.

Many dangers

On their long journey the hawks face many dangers. They travel through unfamiliar territory where they must find food and a sheltered roost. Some starve, misjudge a landing and break a wing, or collide with wires. Others are shot. A few pick up pesticides from their prey; they carry the chemicals in their bodies and later may fail to breed.

Places to watch the spectacle

Strong-flying falcons and buoyant harriers migrate across a broad front—they seldom travel in groups and do not gather at concentration points. Most birds of prey, however, travel along narrow migration routes. Because many birds take the same route, they usually travel in flocks. The flocks join at narrow sea-crossings and mountain ridges, where there is a fairly narrow area with air currents suitable for migration. These are the best places for us to watch and count.

At two known locations, Eilat in Israel and Panama in Central America, more than a million raptors pass each season. Falsterbo in Sweden, Gibraltar at the southern tip of Spain, and the Bosphorus in Turkey are famous places to see large numbers of birds of prey swarming in the air. At Hawk Mountain, Pennsylvania, 7000 hawks were counted passing in a single hour. People watch in thousands; they sit with cameras, binoculars, and telescopes.

CANADA

USA

Broad-winged hawks spend four months in their breeding area.

West Indies

Migration takes about a month.

PANAMA

They spend about seven months in north and central South America, their non-breeding area.

SOUTH AMERICA

Scale

| 0 | 1000 | 2000 kilometers |

| 0 | 620 | 1240 miles |

▲ *Almost all the migrating raptors that leave North America to spend winter in South America pass through Panama. At one point they concentrate in a line only about 5 kilometers (3 miles) wide.*

All Broad-winged Hawks leave their breeding grounds in eastern North America and migrate to Central America and northern South America. Between their breeding and wintering areas, in the balmy West Indies, there is another population of Broad-winged Hawks that have no need to migrate.

Hawk Mountain

Hawk Mountain Sanctuary, Pennsylvania, is the most famous place in North America to watch hawks on migration. In fall, thousands of raptors fly low over the mountain. Once they were shot for "sport". Now crowds of people come to watch the wonderful spectacle and help count the hawks. Different species migrate at slightly different times, so September is the best time for some species, and October or November for others.

Why migrate, and how?

One of the great advantages of flight is that it allows birds to travel far and fast. An area that has plenty of food and places to nest during the breeding season may be inhospitable during the non-breeding season. So some birds of prey take to the air and travel thousands of miles to more pleasant places. To make the journey easier, many catch rides on air-currents.

Follow food

Birds of prey migrate to places where food is better at that time of year. The best-known migrations are from parts of the Northern Hemisphere where the winters are hard. But raptors, and their prey, may also move to avoid extremes of heat and wet.

Difficult decision

Hawks must "decide" whether to stay in their breeding grounds for the winter or to leave. If they stay they may have to cope with the cold, and they may find prey is scarce. If they migrate they must face the hazards of a long journey over unknown terrain.

To avoid the hard winter, Peregrine Falcons (and their prey) leave the tundra of North America. The falcons travel all the way to southern South America, where food is plentiful because it's summer in the Southern Hemisphere. By contrast, many Gyrfalcons stay. Because they are bigger, they withstand the cold better than Peregrines. And they eat Ptarmigan (a species of game bird), which also stay.

W. Perry Conway/Tom Stack & Associates

Follow grasshoppers from USA to SA

From April to September Swainson's Hawks live and breed in the grasslands of western USA. Then most of them travel to South America. The trip of 10 700 kilometers (6600 miles) takes just under two months. On the way, and in South America, flocks feed at grasshopper swarms. Each hawk eats as many as 100 grasshoppers a day.

Neal Smith

◀ *Each fall, almost all Swainson's Hawks leave their breeding grounds in western USA and migrate to Uruguay and Argentina in South America. They pass through Panama, where up to 300 000 have been counted in the sky.*

Soaring or flapping flight?

Most migratory raptors are soarers; they use air-currents rather than powered flight. Swainson's Hawk is a typical soarer. On migration, flocks roost for the night on a hillside. At about 9 or 10 am, warm air currents begin to form, and the hawks take to the air. In high wind or heavy rain they remain at the roost. In the rainy season (September–November) they may take three days to cross Panama on their way to South America. But on the return trip in the dry season they can cross Panama in a day.

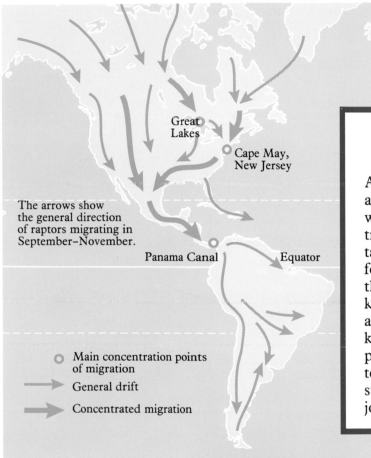

Great Lakes

Cape May, New Jersey

The arrows show the general direction of raptors migrating in September–November.

Panama Canal

Equator

○ Main concentration points of migration

→ General drift

⇒ Concentrated migration

David A. Ponton

▲ *Zone-tailed Hawks, recognized from the white bands across their tails, leave the deserts of south-western USA and follow narrow migration routes to South America. A few remain in the USA for the winter.*

Tracking from a light plane

At South Padre Island, Texas, a migrating Peregrine Falcon was captured. A small radio-transmitter was attached to its tail. Biologists in a light plane followed the falcon overland, through Mexico. It flew 257 kilometers (160 miles) a day, at an average speed of 33 kilometers per hour (20 miles per hour). Each night it landed to rest about two hours before sunset. At 7 am it continued its journey to South America.

Neal Smith

▶ *In fall, Broad-winged Hawks, Swainson's Hawks, Turkey Vultures, Plumbeous Kites, and Mississippi Kites escape the cold North American winter. About a million have been counted as they pass through the Isthmus of Panama in a narrow stream less than 40 kilometers (25 miles) wide. If they do not fly too high, the species can be identified by their different shapes.*

A free ride saves energy

Most birds of prey do not store fat to fuel their migration, and many have little to eat on their long journey. One reason they can do this is that they soar and glide rather than actively fly (flapping). On migration, almost all birds of prey use rising columns of hot air (thermals). Carried in a spiral up these "bird elevators", the hawks use little of their valuable energy. When the thermal runs out, they peel off in the direction of their migration and glide to the next thermal. They travel lowest in the morning and evening, and highest around midday when the thermals are strongest.

Helpful air currents

A thermal is a column of hot air, which rises from ground warmed by the sun. Soaring birds make thermals visible (so do dust devils). The air spirals up the edges of the column until it cools. Hot air rises faster than a non-flapping bird sinks (from gravity). For example, a thermal may rise at 2.1 meters (7 feet) every second while a bird sinks at 1 meter (3.3 feet) per second. Thus, the bird gains height at 1.1 meters (3.6 feet) per second. It controls its flight by opening and closing its wings and tail.

Migrating raptors also follow some mountain ridges and shorelines where wind is deflected upwards to form an updraft. The hawks catch the updrafts for an easy ride. If they can locate a thermal "street" they are swept along for ages.

Studying migration, saving lives

Before 1984 there were dozens of collisions between Israeli military aircraft (patrolling their narrow country) and raptors. Migrating birds were sucked into engines or smashed through windscreens. They caused expensive damage to the planes, and pilots lost their lives. Experts studied the movements of the raptors: the route they took, the height they traveled, and the time of year they came through Israel. The airforce altered its flights to avoid the passing raptor flocks. Since then there has been no serious damage.

Flying with the birds

One of the ways they studied the migrants was in a glider. A flock of about 2000 Honey Buzzards was located from the ground by radar, and two lucky scientists in a motorized glider flew up to join the flock. After they entered the thermal with the buzzards they switched off the glider's motor. They glided in near-silence, with only the sound of air rushing over wings and the sight of buzzards flying, unafraid, a short distance away.

They traveled at heights between 650 and 1500 meters (2130–4900 feet), rising with one thermal then losing height as they glided to the next. In less than 3½ hours they had flown almost the length of Israel, 186 kilometers (115 miles).

▲ *To the prophets of the Old Testament the impressive migration of raptors over the Sinai and the Red Sea was a sign of the mysterious ways of God. Today we understand the movement much better.*

▼ *Hawks on migration gather at points where the crossing is shortest, such as near Istanbul, Turkey. They rise up in one thermal (rising column of air) or updraft, then glide, losing height, to the next.*

▲ *Each fall, the entire population of the Western Honey Buzzards migrates from the breeding grounds in Europe and western Asia to Africa. They return in spring.*

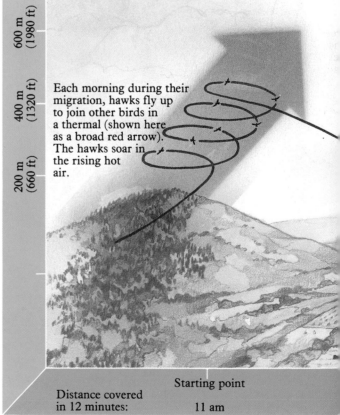

Each morning during their migration, hawks fly up to join other birds in a thermal (shown here as a broad red arrow). The hawks soar in the rising hot air.

600 m (1980 ft)

400 m (1320 ft)

200 m (660 ft)

Starting point

Distance covered in 12 minutes:

11 am

▶ Many raptors that breed at high latitudes across Europe and Asia escape the hard winter and travel to the milder climates of Africa and South-east Asia.

The numbers of migrating hawks can be staggering. In one week about 68 600 Steppe Eagles crossed the Red Sea to Africa at Bab-al-Mandab. There the sea is only 22 kilometers (13½ miles) wide.

Guy Robbrecht/Bruce Coleman Ltd

▲ The Honey Buzzard feeds on the honeycomb and grubs of bees, wasps, and hornets. It escapes the cold winter of its breeding grounds by migrating; 6600 were counted passing through Istanbul on one day, August 29, 1968. At Eilat during one spring, 226 000 were counted returning from Africa.

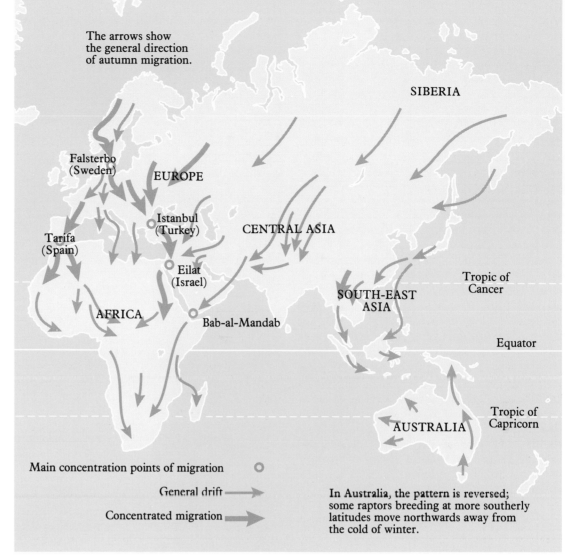

The arrows show the general direction of autumn migration.

SIBERIA

Falsterbo (Sweden)

EUROPE

Istanbul (Turkey)

CENTRAL ASIA

Tarifa (Spain)

Eilat (Israel)

AFRICA

Bab-al-Mandab

SOUTH-EAST ASIA

Tropic of Cancer

Equator

Tropic of Capricorn

AUSTRALIA

Main concentration points of migration ○

General drift →

Concentrated migration ⇒

In Australia, the pattern is reversed; some raptors breeding at more southerly latitudes move northwards away from the cold of winter.

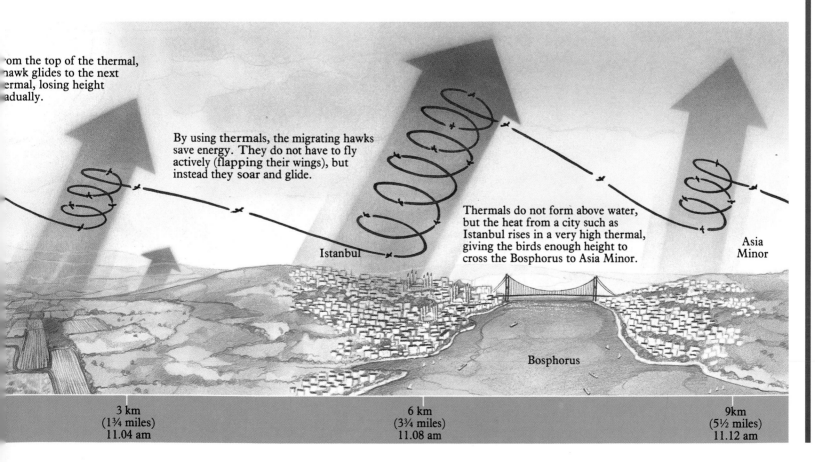

...om the top of the thermal, ...hawk glides to the next ...ermal, losing height ...adually.

By using thermals, the migrating hawks save energy. They do not have to fly actively (flapping their wings), but instead they soar and glide.

Thermals do not form above water, but the heat from a city such as Istanbul rises in a very high thermal, giving the birds enough height to cross the Bosphorus to Asia Minor.

Istanbul

Asia Minor

Bosphorus

3 km (1¾ miles) 11.04 am

6 km (3¾ miles) 11.08 am

9km (5½ miles) 11.12 am

Three South American hawks

A wide variety of birds of prey is found in South America. Some are threatened with extinction. For timber, humans cut down the trees that provide the hawks with food, shelter, and nest-sites. Elsewhere, in farmland, the hawks are shot because they kill poultry and other livestock.

Common: The Red-backed Hawk is quite numerous. It is a strong hunter and eats many birds. It also uses a wide variety of nest-sites: rock ledges, telephone poles, grass tussocks, and trees. Because it is so adaptable it can live well in many places.

Rare: The closely related Galapagos Hawk is just as strong and adaptable. It feeds on whatever meat it can find. Unfortunately many are shot because they eat poultry. Cats were introduced to some of the Galapagos Islands, and they eat hawk chicks. Because the islands are small and isolated there were never many hawks. Now there are fewer than 200 pairs left. Fortunately they are surviving well on the islands where no humans live.

In trouble: The Slate-colored Hawk has short wings suited to life in the forest. It is thought to live around rivers and streams and feed on frogs and snakes. It was once quite common, but now, because humans are destroying its forests, it is disappearing.

Eric & David Hosking

▲ *Almost nothing is known about the Slate-colored Hawk from the forests of Amazonia.*

Godfrey Merlen/Oxford Scientific Films

▶ *Where wind hits lava ridges and is deflected upwards, Galapagos Hawks often hover. They peer down, inspecting the ground for lizards and other prey. In a stiff breeze they do not need to flap, but hang with wings spread, their tips bent up by the wind currents. The Red-backed Hawk uses the same hunting method.*

◀ *The Red-backed Hawk hunts in open country, from Colombia to Patagonia, and on the Falkland Islands. It eats wild guinea pigs, but in farmland it catches domestic animals—here, a goose.*

▶ *These adult Galapagos Hawks have captured a young marine iguana. They also eat giant centipedes, lizards, snakes, seabird chicks, turtles, and offal.* **The hawk is amazingly tame, probably because it has had little contact with humans. To take a photo you simply walk up to one with a camera.**

Frans Lanting/Minden Pictures

Q. Why do birds of prey hover?

A. Hovering gives the hawk a good view of the ground below, rather like a perch in the air. The hawk's head stays still while its body, wings, and tail shift about and take the buffets of the wind. By keeping its head still, the hawk can fix its eyes on prey. Once prey is spotted the hawk descends, perhaps stopping once or twice to check its position, then it drops onto the prey.

Fabulous fisher

The Osprey catches live fish near the water's surface. It has a number of odd features that help it to catch, grip, and eat this tough, slippery prey. And what a spectacular diver it is!

Active fishers

Even ornithologists, who spend hours studying birds, rarely see raptors make a kill. With Ospreys, however, once you know where they hunt regularly, you can watch from the waterside. It can be an exciting experience, particularly if they dive.

An Osprey is an active hunter; it searches out prey rather than perching and waiting. It flies slowly, often in a circle, usually up to 40 meters (130 feet) above the water. Sometimes it hovers. Finally it swoops and snatches a fish, or it plunges. As the bird nears the fish it thrusts its legs forward in line with its head. This is rather like sighting prey down the barrel of a rifle.

The water distorts its view, but the Osprey allows for this. It hits with toes open, and they close automatically. They snap shut incredibly fast, in two-hundredths of a second! The Osprey aligns the captured fish with its body, like a torpedo, and flies to a perch to eat. On the way it may shake the water from its feathers; like a wet dog, its head stays steady but its body swivels from side to side.

How good at fishing is it?

Fish up to 3 kilograms (6½ pounds), but usually less than 250 grams (9 ounces), are almost all the Osprey eats. Hunting success depends on a number of things such as the experience of the bird, the weather, and the type of fish. Sometimes Ospreys are successful in as few as 30 per cent of their attempts to catch fish; at other times the success rate may be 90 per cent. They have more success catching slow-moving fish than fast divers. Young Ospreys are about half as successful as adults and must hunt longer each day.

In the non-breeding season the Osprey may spend only half an hour to catch enough to eat for the day. A breeding male Osprey must hunt a lot longer; he has to feed himself, his female, and any chicks. He might spend one-quarter of the daylight hours hunting on the wing.

Nest in colonies

In many but not all parts of the world, Ospreys breed in colonies. Whale Island, Mexico, has one of the densest colonies: there are 110 pairs nesting per square kilometer. Baja California is another good breeding area with no mammal predators to rob the eggs or chicks of the ground-nesting Ospreys. There the nests are about 100 meters (330 feet) apart.

Helping each other to find fish

At some breeding colonies where Ospreys hunt not far from the nests, males arriving back with school-fish arrive noisily. Other males then head off in the direction from which the

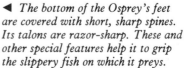

◄ *The bottom of the Osprey's feet are covered with short, sharp spines. Its talons are razor-sharp. These and other special features help it to grip the slippery fish on which it preys.*

Keith Scholey/Planet Earth Pictures

Huge nests

Generations of Ospreys have added to this sturdy nest piled on a beach. It is perhaps 1 meter (3¼ feet) high and 2.5 meters (8 feet) across. This year's pair of birds need to do only a few repairs and add a fresh lining of seaweed or moss.

successful birds arrived. They too soon return with a school fish each. If a male comes in with a non-schooling fish it arrives quietly, and others don't head off. In this case, it's not worthwhile for other males to fly off in the direction indicated by the returning hunter. It would not help them to find fish.

Where the land meets the water

Ospreys are almost worldwide in distribution. However, in Africa south of the Sahara Desert, and in South America, they are migrants from Europe and North America, and do not breed there. Ospreys in Australia breed and do not migrate. They are found near relatively calm, clear water on sea coasts, rivers, and lakes.

▼ *After seven or more weeks in the nest these Osprey chicks will be ready to make their first flight. By then they will be as big as their parents. They grow remarkably quickly.*

◄ *No other bird is quite like the Osprey. It has long narrow wings with a very flexible carpal joint (at the bend in the wing). When the Osprey dives after fish, the joint allows it to sweep its wing forward and back, and lift clear of the water.*
To help it grip and carry wriggling, slimy fish, it can turn its outer toe back so that it has two toes back, and two forward. (All other birds of prey have three forward, one back.) In a dive, it can close its slit-like nostril to keep out water.

Nellaine Price/Survival Anglia

Strange falcons

Despite appearances, caracaras belong to the same family of birds as the typical falcons. The family Falconidae has about 60 species, distributed around the world. It includes falcons, falconets, and caracaras. The greatest number of species is found in South America.

Family Falconidae

Caracaras, milvagos, forest falcons, falconets, and true falcons belong to a group of related species, called a family—the family Falconidae. They are distributed worldwide, and have hooked beaks and curved talons.

All species in this family share some distinct features in their skeleton. When their eggs are blown (emptied), and held up to the light, the shell is brownish inside, rather than greenish like the hawks' eggs. (Hawks belong to the family Accipitridae.) They all molt their wing feathers in the same order, but differently from the way that hawks molt.

Caracaras

There are about eight species of caracara, all in Central and South America. The name "caracara" describes the bird's call. It is a cackling cry usually made with the head

Striated Caracara

Identification of the Striated Caracara is easy. Where it is found, there is nothing similar to confuse it with. As an adult it is black with white streaks on the breast, a white tip to the tail, and characteristic rufous (red) thighs.

▼ *A Striated Caracara on the Falkland Islands. Penguins (upper right corner of photo) and albatrosses return to the islands each year to breed. The caracara scrounges around their colonies in search of chicks and scraps.*
The caracara's unusual orange crop sticks out of its dark chest feathers. It is very obvious when full of food. Perhaps it advertises the fact that the bird has just fed.

thrown back, mostly in the early morning or late evening during breeding season.

The Striated Caracara lives in tussock grassland and barren country on the Falkland Islands and small islands off the tip of South America. A medium-sized bird, it is one of the larger species in the falconid family.

The wings of the Striated Caracara are quite long and pointed, like typical falcons. Yet it hardly lives up to the image of a noble falcon. It has a rather weak beak, and talons made for walking and digging rather than gripping and killing. It eats carrion and is a rather sluggish flier. It spends a lot of time on the ground and can run well.

Scratching and scavenging

The Striated Caracara mostly scavenges (eats dead animals and other meat scraps). At seabird colonies it feasts on dead chicks and adults. With sturdy legs and quite flat claws, it scratches the soil for beetles and grubs. It lifts bark and upturns cowpats to feed on the

insects living there. When the seabirds finish breeding and leave for the winter, the Striated Caracara goes beachcombing. It searches the shoreline for marine life washed in by the tide.

Occasionally, it attacks sick or weak animals, even those as big as sheep. Because of its habit of eating lambs and disabled sheep, farmers have shot many caracaras—so many that the birds do well only on uninhabited islands, where people do not graze their livestock.

Ground-nester

In summer (which in the Southern Hemisphere is December, January, and February) the Striated Caracara lays two or three eggs in a smallish nest it builds from tussock grass and stems, sometimes lined with wool. Several pairs may nest as close as 6 meters (20 feet) apart, amongst the tussock grass or on rocky ledges. The eggs hatch in December. The chicks have unusual orange-tan down (soft baby feathers). In March the fledglings seem to become independent of their parents.

By their fifth year the fledglings will have changed from black with brown markings to the colors of an adult. In the adult the brown on the chest and tail tip has changed to gray-white. The legs are a rich red-brown, and the bare skin of the face, legs and crop has turned from gray to a striking orange-yellow.

▼ *Immature caracaras have a tug-of-war over a scrap of food. Squabbles are frequent, but real fights are rare. The birds usually work out their differences in other ways.*

▲ *One caracara, on the right, its beak held up in threat, is bothering the other. In response, the other throws back its head and calls a high screech over and over.*

Fabulous falcons

Falcons are much admired for their beauty and sensational hunting skills. However, they do vary greatly in appearance and habits. The Peregrine Falcon is one of the most spectacular of all raptors, and it has had a long association with humans. The relationship has not always been good, but it has never been dull.

Typical falcons

The typical falcons are small to medium-sized raptors, with compact bodies and long, pointed wings. Females are larger than males—sometimes much larger.

Because they are quite variable, it is hard to describe a typical falcon. Although falcons are well known for their swift powerful flight, some species are slower fliers, and hoverers. Many, but not all, catch other birds in the air after a spectacular chase. Others prefer to attack ground-living prey (e.g. the Saker Falcon); some eat insects (the Lesser Kestrel), or lizards (the Mauritius Kestrel), or even carrion (the Brown Falcon).

Although falcons typically prefer open habitats, some live in forest (e.g. the Mauritius Kestrel). Most nest as solitary pairs, but a few nest in colonies (the Lesser Kestrel).

Generally the female falcon incubates the eggs and tends the young, and the male supplies the food. None of the falcons build their own nest. They nest in a hollow tree, a rock ledge, or a stick-nest built by another species. They lay a clutch of two to six eggs. Some species have a fairly fixed clutch size, but others lay more eggs when food is abundant than when it is scarce. Incubation takes about four or four and a half weeks. The chicks of small species are in the nest for about four weeks. For larger falcon species this period is six and a half weeks.

Most spectacular, most admired

The Peregrine is everything a falcon is supposed to be: bold and beautiful, with superb powers of flight. It is one of the fastest of birds and a spectacular hunter. For centuries

▲ *Chicks being kept warm in a brooder.*

▲ *Chicks being fed by a person wearing a glove-puppet. Can you see the person's fingers in the shadow under the neck of the puppet?*

Raised by humans

In recent years, many raptors have been bred in captivity. They are bred for release, to build up wild populations of rare species; for research; or for falconry. More Peregrine Falcons have been bred in captivity than any other raptor, not because they are easy to breed but because an enormous effort has gone into developing the best techniques. First, the adult birds are encouraged to lay many eggs, and these are put in an incubator. After hatching, groups of chicks are kept warm in brooders. In the wild, chicks quickly learn to respond to the head pattern of their parent. This is called "imprinting", and later it helps them to recognize their own species. In captivity, a puppet step-mother (with the correct pattern) is used to feed the chicks. If humans fed them directly, it could cause problems when they are ready to breed: they might look for a human mate rather than a falcon.

How fast?

Everyone wants to know which bird is the fastest. Some think it is the Peregrine Falcon. In a stoop (a breathtaking dive) the falcon may reach 180 kilometers per hour (112 miles per hour). In steady level flight the falcon is not as fast, and there are a few birds that can outfly it. Some books claim higher speeds, such as 320 km/h (200 mph), but they may be exaggerated. It is hard to measure the speed of a bird. Radar has recently been used to get accurate cruising (steady flying) speeds: Ospreys cruised at 47 km/h (29 mph), Eurasian Sparrowhawks at 43 km/h (27 mph), and Old World Kestrels at 32 km/h (20 mph).

The Peregrine Falcon. Its typical shape when gliding is shown above.

it has been admired by poets, artists, and nature-lovers. It is the choice of falconers around the world.

Most widely distributed, most famous

The Peregrine Falcon is found almost everywhere in the world—probably the most widely distributed of any bird. It breeds almost anywhere except the highest mountains, the driest deserts, Antarctica, and some rainforests and oceanic islands.

In the 1960s and 1970s the Peregrine began disappearing from vast areas. Organochlorine pesticides were eventually found to be the cause, and they were banned, or their use restricted, in many parts of the world.

The effort to find the connection between pesticides and Peregrines brought a lot of different people together. It drew attention to the harmful effects of pesticides and how they had spread everywhere around the world. This made the Peregrine famous, a symbol of environmental conservation. Now the Peregrine has returned to many of its former nesting places, and it has achieved more fame as a great conservation success.

Most persecuted

Until the end of the eighteenth century, falconry was the main way for rich land-owners to catch game-birds. Then they began to use guns for this sport, and Peregrine Falcons became competitors with humans for game-birds. Many Peregrines were shot on grouse moors and around the lofts of racing pigeons. Even today a few owners of racing pigeons blame Peregrines for all their pigeon losses, and they kill them (illegally) at every opportunity.

The Peregrine's taste for pigeons also caused trouble in Britain during the Second World War. Pigeons were used to carry important military messages, particularly from pilots when they crash-landed. Destruction of eggs and falcons was allowed in many parts of England; and the Peregrine populations in parts of the south coast were wiped out. However, the damage wasn't permanent, and soon after the war the Peregrines were back.

Ringed for life

All around the world, thousands of Peregrine Falcon chicks have been ringed at their nests. Each ring, or band, has an individual number, plus a return address in case the bird is found at a later date. Recovery of any ringed individuals, months or years later, gives us information about how long they live, whether they move around, and other useful facts.

Stephen J Krasemann/Bruce Coleman Ltd

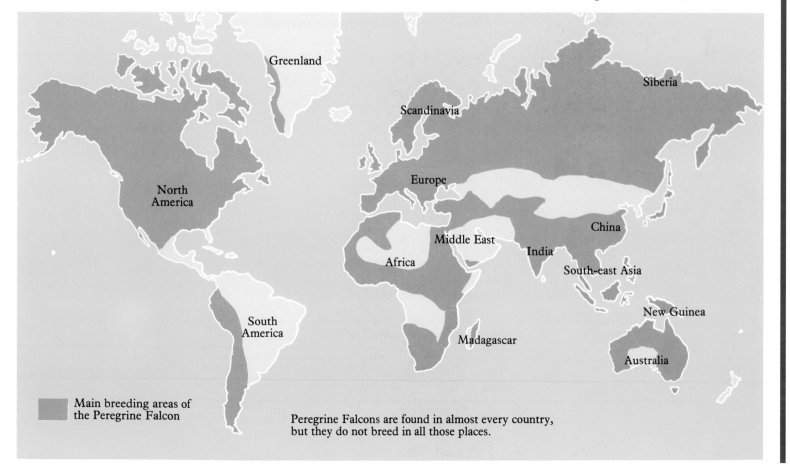

Greenland

Siberia

Scandinavia

Europe

North America

China

Middle East

India

Africa

South-east Asia

South America

New Guinea

Madagascar

Australia

Main breeding areas of the Peregrine Falcon

Peregrine Falcons are found in almost every country, but they do not breed in all those places.

Hands-on help

Return of the Peregrine

When pesticides wiped out all the Peregrine Falcons breeding east of the Mississippi River in the United States, and left only a few pairs in the western states, a rescue program was begun in 1970 by "The Peregrine Fund".

Captive-bred chicks have been released using two main methods. Where breeding pairs remain, their eggs, if damaged by pesticides, are replaced with three-week-old chicks. This is known as fostering.

Where there are no breeders, a medieval technique called "hacking back" is used. Huge office blocks replace the castle turrets of medieval times or the natural cliff sites of Peregrines. Chicks are released high on the building and gradually become independent. After wandering for a year or two, some may return to office blocks to breed. In 1990 there were at least 32 new pairs of Peregrines in 24 North American cities.

Given a second chance

Raptor rehabilitation centers have been created all around the USA. Raptors found sick, injured, or orphaned are treated and, if possible, released back to the wild for a second chance. Most casualties are due to humans: cars, wires, shotguns. The centers help to offset that loss, and their efforts demonstrate the value that is placed on raptors today.

Stephen J. Krasemann/Bruce Coleman Ltd

Detective work

Many Peregrine Falcons are trapped, by biologists, at the nest or during migration. They are weighed and measured, and a ring is put on their leg. The length of their wing can give a clue to where they come from. The falcons do not enjoy being handled, but they are released unharmed and the information gained is of great value.

Frans Lanting/Minden Pictures

▲ *High on office buildings, Peregrine Falcon chicks are released to build up the wild population. A technique called "hacking back" is used. Before they can fly, the chicks are placed in a wire-fronted box with a good view. After a while they are released. They return to the box for food less and less, over perhaps six weeks, as they develop the hunting skills to feed themselves.*

David A. Ponton

◀ *This immature Peregrine Falcon is known as AJ6. The letters on its leg band are visible through a telescope. They will identify this bird if it is found dead, in trouble, or, best of all, breeding at some later date.*

Seldom sick

Birds of prey are rarely found sick in the wild. However, like all birds, they carry parasites. (A parasite is an animal or plant that lives on another animal.) External parasites include the biting louse. Lice can cause skin irritation and feather damage, but to a healthy bird they are seldom a problem. Avian pox is nastier. It is a viral infection that causes ugly sores on parts of the bird where there are no feathers. Some birds recover. Others die, particularly those that cannot hunt because the scabs cover their eyes. The wild Peregrine Falcon in the photo on the left was brought to a rehabilitation center for help.

▲ *A biting louse (photographically enlarged), which lives among the feathers.*

Peregrine: king of falcons

The Peregrine has sharp senses to find prey and powerful weapons to overcome prey. It must be the finest of bird hunters. Unfortunately it has been badly affected by persistent pesticides, which it accumulates from its prey, eventually acquiring a greater amount than most other birds.

Bird-eater

The Peregrine Falcon eats other birds. It takes an enormous variety of species, from tiny sparrows to large geese. Male Peregrines tend to eat smaller prey than females do. Both prefer doves and pigeons wherever they are available.

Typically, the Peregrine catches prey in the air. However, it sometimes catches ground-dwellers: rabbits, lemmings, and ground birds. Occasionally it takes bats. Young Peregrines, especially, eat flying insects.

High hunter

From a perch high on a cliff, the Peregrine swoops down at passing flocks of birds. It waits until the birds are away from cover before launching its attack. At times it will "ring up" with a flock. The falcon follows the flock upwards, while the flock tries to stay safely above the falcon. They may climb to 1000 meters (3300 feet) in the air. Eventually one bird may panic and drop. The falcon stoops after it; the chase is breathtaking.

Q. Falcons don't have teeth, do they?

A. Yes! Falcons do have teeth, known as tomial teeth. They are not like our teeth though. They are projections in the upper mandible (beak), one on each side. If prey is not dead from the impact of the falcon's strike, then the falcon bites its neck to kill it. The teeth are thought to help snap the neck of prey. They keep the prey in the front of the beak and stop it from slipping back, where the falcon could not bite as effectively.

N.N. Birks

Speed and surprise: a deadly combination

The Peregrine may approach its prey as if out of the sun, or by sweeping low, then up and over a building. Either way, the prey doesn't see the falcon until it is too late to escape. A falcon's stoop also has an element of surprise in it. The falcon rockets down out of nowhere. It has such a great advantage in speed that the prey has no chance to reach shelter.

Hit and miss

The falcon usually hits its prey with its feet, before sweeping up and back to catch the dead or stunned bird as it falls. A puff of feathers often signals a hit. Occasionally the falcon "binds" (holds on) to a bird as it hits it.

Even Peregrines miss occasionally. Their hunting success varies from about 1 in 10 birds attacked, to 9 in 10. Success depends on many things. Generally, it is easier to catch a tired migrating bird, or a young one, than an experienced, well-rested adult bird.

Most studied

The Peregrine must be the most studied of all raptors. This is partly because of the impact that pesticides have had on the falcon. It was studied around the world: first, to establish the cause of the widespread disappearance of breeding pairs; later, to see which populations were affected. It took many years to prove that organochlorine pesticides were the cause of problems.

Pesky pesticides

DDT, aldrin, and dieldrin are very effective pesticides. DDT was first widely used in the late 1940s, and aldrin and dieldrin in the 1950s. Not until the 1960s was it discovered that DDT causes Peregrines to lay eggs with thin shells. Some of the eggs are so thin that they break when the female tries to incubate them. Aldrin and dieldrin are highly toxic, and they kill embryos and adult falcons.

The falcon eats the pesticides in the bodies of its prey. With each step up the food chain— from sprayed grass, to grasshopper, to starling, to falcon—the pesticides get more concentrated. The falcon gets the largest dose of all. Now that these pesticides are banned or restricted in many countries, the numbers of Peregrines are building up again. This is the final proof that pesticides were responsible for the disappearance of Peregrines.

▲ *Peregrine Falcons are powerful hunters. They catch birds in the air after a chase or a stoop (dive). This male Peregrine in Australia has caught a Galah: a parrot roughly half his weight and with a powerful beak that could severely injure him. The female arrives to share the meal.*

◀ *The hard, neat feathers of the Peregrine Falcon, which fit tightly to the body, are designed for swift flight with minimum drag. They are also reasonably waterproof.*

From fluffy chicks to fierce falcons

Peregrine Falcons breed once a year, usually on rugged cliffs. They defend the nest savagely but are gentle parents. The chicks grow amazingly fast and are as big as their parents before they leave the nest at about seven weeks of age. In three years they are generally ready to breed themselves.

Breeding territory

It is mainly the responsibility of the male to set up the breeding territory and defend it from other Peregrines. When there are enough suitable nest-sites, Peregrine pairs space themselves out fairly regularly. Where food is plentiful there may be a Peregrine every 2 kilometers (1¼ miles). Usually they are much further apart.

Generations of Peregrines use the same nest-site year after year. Sites known to sixteenth-century falconers are still in use today. Favored sites are cliffs with grassy ledges or small caves, sheltered from the worst weather; they face the morning sunlight, and ground animals cannot reach them. In some areas where there are no cliffs, the falcon chooses the stick-nest of a raven or a larger raptor or, less often, a large tree-hollow. In a few places the nest will be on the ground.

Courtship

In early spring, before they lay eggs, a pair of Peregrines must strengthen their pair bond, decide on a nest-site, and mate. They do quite a lot of flying displays, especially the male. He also brings food to the female (courtship feeding). The pair perform various courtship displays at the nest. They bow and call excitedly.

Eggs and incubation

The female lays one egg every second day. Clutch size varies: it is usually four eggs in

▲ Female falcons are larger than male falcons. This difference in size between the sexes is known as sexual dimorphism. Bird-eating falcons, such as Peregrine, are usually highly dimorphic. Rodent-eating falcons are moderately dimorphic, and insect-eating falcons only slightly so. In carrion-eating vultures (above, right), the male and female are about the same size.

▲ When mating the male lands on the female's back, with his sharp talons safely clenched.

Male and female co-operate

Peregrine Falcons are monogamous. That is, a male and one female form a pair for breeding. They may stay together for years. They breed once a year.

The pair split nest duties. The larger female incubates the eggs and broods the chicks. Occasionally the male relieves her on the nest. Mostly, the male hunts for the family. He delivers prey to the female, who then tears it up and offers it to the chicks. When the chicks are older the female begins to hunt, and the chicks tear up their own food.

Britain, three in Australia, and three or four in different parts of North America. After laying the second egg the female begins to incubate. She sits for about five weeks.

Hard work hatching

The chick has a special strong muscle on the back of its neck and an egg tooth on its beak. When ready to hatch, it pushes a small section of shell up with its beak; this is called "pipping". The chick works its way around the blunt end of the shell, rather like a can-opener. Over two or three days it cuts the shell almost into two halves and then, with a heave, forces them apart.

Wobbly heads and constant care

Usually two chicks hatch on the same day, then a third chick a day or two later. Their eyes are closed, and they are thinly covered in white down. On their second day they softly "peep" and reach, wobbly headed, towards the sound of their mother, who "chupps" gently as she offers food. The chicks take a tiny sliver or two and then collapse into the nest. By the fourth day their necks are stronger and their eyes are fully open.

The chicks are fed every few hours throughout the day. Sometimes the male catches extra food, which the female stores (caches) in holes in the cliff. Later in the day she feeds it to the chicks. Caching seems to help keep mealtimes fairly regular.

Fat and fluffy

By 14 days the chicks have grown a woolly white down, and they stand strongly. Their mother broods them less because they are able to keep themselves warm. She still covers them at night and shelters them from rain and hot sun.

By three weeks of age they are more difficult to handle, and they cackle, hiss, and strike with their feet at human visitors. Among themselves they squabble a little over food, but nest life is generally peaceful. They can tear food for themselves, but would rather have their mother do it.

First flight

Not all eggs hatch, and not all chicks survive to fledge. The chicks that survive make their first flight from the nest about seven weeks after hatching. Male chicks fledge a few days before the females. Incredibly, they now weigh as much as their parents.

For a month or two they stay in the vicinity of the nest. Their parents feed them less and less as they learn to hunt. In arctic areas, soon after nesting the adults and fledglings migrate.

Some survive to breed

For the first few years of their life the young Peregrines wander. Perhaps as many as two-thirds of them do not survive to breeding age. Females can start breeding at two or three years of age; males at three years of age or older.

▼ *A rocky ledge, overhung from above, makes a sheltered nest. Just a little soil, and scattered feathers from prey, are enough for the female to make a shallow "cup" to hold her eggs and young chicks. This three-week-old brood gather around to take slivers of meat gently offered to them by their parent.*

America: land of eight brave falcons, home of five free falcons

Almost everywhere in the world there is at least one species of falcon. Eight species are found in North America. Two of these, the Northern Hobby and the Old World Kestrel, are only accidental visitors from Europe. A third, the Aplomado Falcon, no longer breeds in the USA. That leaves five regular falcons.

The smallest of the five falcons is the colorful American Kestrel. It is common and is found throughout North America south of the Arctic treeline. The male is 24 centimeters (9½ inches) from the tip of his head to the tip of his tail. The female is 25 centimeters (10 inches) long.

The largest is the magnificent Gyrfalcon; it is also the largest of all the falcons. The male is 52 centimeters (20½ inches) long. The female is 59 centimeters (23 inches) long. Gyrfalcons breed in Arctic regions, including Alaska, but are nowhere common.

Merlins breed in the forests of Alaska and Canada, and on the prairies south to the northern USA. They are dashing little falcons, which hunt birds and insects on the wing. In winter they are widely but sparsely distributed throughout the United States.

There are two middle-sized falcons: the Peregrine Falcon and the Prairie Falcon. The Prairie Falcon is fairly common in hill and mountain grasslands of western USA. It hunts birds and mammals that live on the ground, especially squirrels. The Peregrine can be seen almost anywhere but does not breed in many inland states.

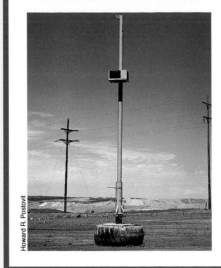

Howard R. Postovit

Conservation

During a break in blasting at a mine in New Mexico, a pair of Prairie Falcons nested on a rock-face. When mining was due to start again, biologists moved the falcon chicks to this box on a modified mobile light pole. At first they left it next to the rock-face. Then, over several days they moved it to a safe distance from the rock wall. The parents continued to feed the chicks, which fledged successfully.

Frans Lanting/Minden Pictures

Frans Lanting/Minden Pictures

▲ *Shorebirds flee in panic as a Merlin sweeps up ready to dive at any vulnerable members of the flock. The Merlin is found across northern North America, and also in Europe and Asia. It has recently moved into the some Canadian cities such as Saskatoon.*

◄ *A Gyrfalcon on its half-eaten kill. It may have been one of a small number that move southwards into the USA for the winter. Gyrfalcons breed in the Arctic tundra and subarctic mountains of Alaska and Canada, where many adults remain for the winter, feeding on Ptarmigan (a kind of grouse).*

◄ *Prairie Falcons nest on bluffs overlooking the dry plains of the American West, from southern Canada to northern Mexico. Some range more widely in winter, into farmlands.*

▲ *Destruction of habitat is the greatest threat to raptors. Preservation of wilderness areas is the best way to conserve many birds of prey.*

Q. Are any North American falcons extinct?

A. No. The Aplomado Falcon no longer occurs in North America as a breeder, although it visits occasionally. Before the 1950s, it bred in savanna grasslands, with cactus and mesquite, in Texas and Arizona. Loss of this habitat seems to be the reason for its disappearance. In an attempt to establish some breeding pairs, biologists are releasing captive-bred birds into part of their former Texas range.

55

Adapting to change

The Old World Kestrel is Europe's best-known and most common bird of prey. It even lives in cities. Because it uses a wide variety of nest-sites and prey types, it can adapt to change. Few birds of prey are as adaptable as this.

Many types of nest-sites

Sheltered ledges or holes are this kestrel's favorite nest-sites. They can be in cliffs; in quarries and old pipes; on church towers and ruins; or high-rise buildings and bridges. Stick-nests of crows and natural tree-hollows are also suitable. In war-torn areas kestrels happily use holes in the walls of buildings that have been blasted by shells.

City slickers

Because the kestrel nests on tall buildings, the Germans call it the *Turmfalke* ("tower falcon"). City kestrels must put up with a lot of disturbance; they raise chicks on the balconies of apartments and the ledges of busy office buildings. They thrive in the city, as long as there is open space where they can hunt, among the concrete canyons.

In England, London is the last place you would think to look for kestrels. Yet a survey in 1967 located about 142 pairs of kestrels within 30 kilometers (18½ miles) of St Paul's Cathedral. Most lived in and around parks; some were near docks and factories.

Adaptable predator

If the kestrel is not too fussy about where it nests, it is not picky about what it eats either. Its main prey are small mammals such as mice and voles. But it can also catch and eat a variety of other animals, including bats, birds, reptiles, frogs, insects, and earthworms.

George I. Bernard/Oxford Scientific Films

Q. Why do many falcons have a dark streak under each eye?

A. Nobody knows for sure. Some people think that it helps to reduce the amount of glare reaching the eye, so that the falcon can see more easily in bright light. Football players sometimes paint black under their eyes for the same reason.

◀ *The Old World Kestrel may be the most numerous of all birds of prey. It is found in Europe, Asia, and Africa. Although cities have been built in former kestrel country, some kestrels have moved back there. Antennas make handy perches.*

Changing attitudes, helping hawks

Once, countless Australian raptors were shot, poisoned, or trapped because they were "killers", blamed for stealing chickens and killing lambs. But research has shown that, in general, even the larger birds of prey do little harm to livestock. Environmental education has helped people to understand the role of raptors in nature. Raptors are now fully protected by law in Australia. That means it is illegal to kill them or take their eggs. In recent years, attitudes have changed so much that many people now feel proud to have a raptor living near them.

More kestrel country

Humans have changed much of the Australian landscape, often with disastrous results for the wildlife. In general, raptors are less numerous in places that are used intensively by humans. However, there are exceptions: partial clearing of forests for grazing and agriculture, and building of dams inland, have opened up new land for the kestrel. The kestrel eats mice and locusts; both are pests of crops, so this helps farmers.

Rabbits: a mixed blessing

In the nineteeth century rabbits were brought to Australia and released into the wild. They spread over half the country and badly affected the survival of many native mammals. For some raptors this was a blessing—they fed easily on rabbits. Now in many areas rabbit is an important part of the diet of goshawks and Brown Falcons. Starlings, which also came from Europe, are another mixed blessing: they take nest hollows from native birds, but many raptors eat starlings.

John Kiely/Australasian Nature Transparencies

▲ *This little kestrel has been trapped for research. It will be released unharmed. Several decades ago, even kestrels were trapped to be killed because of a mistaken belief that all birds of prey killed livestock.*

Thirsty?

Because they get water from the moist meat they eat, birds of prey don't need to drink as much as many other birds. But they do drink occasionally, especially when it is hot. They scoop water into the lower beak, tip the head back, and let the water run down the throat. Some other birds can suck water up, like we can.

David Hollands

► *For some Australian raptors, the introduced rabbit has become an important prey. Brown Falcons catch many small rabbits.*

Falco in the African region

Eighteen species, about half of all the falcons, are found in Africa. Thirteen breed there, and five visit as migrants. Another four species are found on neighboring islands. No other region has so much good falcon country and so many falcons. Nevertheless, some of the falcons have special needs.

Falco

Falco sounds like a robot crime-fighter in a cartoon. It is the generic name for all the typical falcons, of which there are 36 to 38 species. The name means "a sickle" and refers to falcons' curved claws.

In addition to the 18 falcons found in Africa, another four occur on the neighboring islands of Madagascar, Mauritius, and the Seychelles. The ecological conditions in Africa—miles and miles of tropical steppe, savanna and woodland—obviously suit falcons very well. Some species, however, have very particular requirements.

African Pygmy Falcon: depends on weaverbirds

Pygmy falcons are not typical falcons (they are not in the genus *Falco*) but are close relatives. There are only two pygmy falcons (genus *Polihierax*): one in Africa, one in Asia.

The African Pygmy Falcon lives year-round in dry thornbush and scrub in two separate parts of Africa. In southern Africa it is found wherever there are Social Weavers; in north-eastern Africa it depends on the White-headed Buffalo Weaver.

Weaverbirds provide the falcon with a place to roost and nest. The Sociable Weaver builds an enormous nest of grass, with a number of nest chambers in the underside, in a thorn tree. About 25 per cent of Sociable Weaver nests have a resident falcon. The weaver and falcon breed at different times, so there is very little conflict about the nest. Perhaps the weavers are helped by the aggressive little falcon who guards their nest. However, the falcon is not always grateful for a place to nest, as it occasionally eats Sociable Weavers.

▼ *Unusual pale eyes immediately distinguish the White-eyed Kestrel from the other kestrels. It lives in dry open country, from Somalia to the Transvaal in Africa.*

◄ *The African Pygmy Falcon, with hooked beak, strong feet, and sharp talons, is a tiny copy of the larger falcons. This is a female; males have a gray back.*

Perfect miniatures

One of the smallest raptors is the African Pygmy Falcon (shown here). It is closely related to the two smallest: the tiny Black-thighed and Bornean Falconets. Both are found in South-east Asia and are bold hunters of insects and, perhaps, small birds. About 12 centimeters in length (4¾ inches) and 35 grams (1¼ ounces) in weight, they are only slightly bigger than a House Sparrow.

White-eyed kestrel: depends on rooks

The White-eyed Kestrel is distributed largely where there are Cape Rooks, in scattered parts of eastern and southern Africa. It nests in stick-nests built by the rook. Powerlines have allowed both the rook and the kestrel to nest in treeless places, which previously had no nest-sites.

The White-eyed Kestrel lives in low-rainfall grassland with patches of bare ground. It hunts mainly insects but also small birds, mammals, and reptiles. In some places it is nomadic: when conditions are good, several arrive, breed, then depart. Elsewhere, pairs nest about 3 kilometers (2 miles) apart, in the same area year after year. There is lots of suitable habitat in Africa for the White-eyed Kestrel. Why the kestrel doesn't use it all is a mystery.

Sooty falcon: depends on migrant birds

The Sooty Falcon breeds in the Libyan Desert and islands in the Red Sea and Persian Gulf. It nests in dry, bare areas: on rocky outcrops among the desert sand; and coral cliffs and small rocky islands. In the desert it nests solitarily (isolated pairs), but on islands it nests in colonies of perhaps 100 pairs, each pair about 45 meters (150 feet) apart.

In such barren areas there is not much prey. However, each year a stream of migrant birds passes over, heading for Africa for the winter. The Sooty Falcon has timed its breeding so that it can feed its chicks on the tired bee-eaters, hoopoes, orioles, and warblers that pass.

In late October the falcons begin to depart for a very different habitat in eastern Africa and Madagascar. They migrate, often in small flocks, to the same areas each year. On the way they feed on swarming insects such as termites, locusts, and dragonflies, and bats. They stay in moist savannas and the edge of forests in Madagascar until February.

Mauritius Kestrel: depends on forest

The Mauritius Kestrel is an unusual falcon: it has short rounded wings (perfect for life in the forest) and eats finger-length geckos. It was widely distributed over the island of Mauritius, once home to the extinct Dodo. Now more than 85 per cent of the forest has been cleared, and few kestrels remain. However, some have recently been bred in captivity and released in farmlands with trees, where they are breeding successfully. So although the Mauritius Kestrel is still the rarest falcon in the world, it is no longer the rarest raptor.

Peter Steyn

▲ *The Mauritius Kestrel is the rarest falcon in the world; in the 1970s only about three pairs were known to survive. Habitat loss, pesticides, persecution, and predation of eggs and nestlings by monkeys have all been suggested as possible causes. The release of captive-bred birds has helped to build up the wild population.*

Q. Why does a falcon bob its head?

A. Perched falcons bob their heads up and down when they see something of interest. The movements look cute, but because each eye sights the object of interest from a number of different angles, they improve the raptor's three-dimensional vision and enable it to judge distance more accurately.

▶ *Sooty Falcons breed in the dry treeless Sahara Desert and the Near East, where they live on migrating birds. By November they have migrated to the grasslands and forest edges of eastern Africa and Madagascar, where they eat insects.*

O. Langrano/Bruce Coleman Ltd

Hawks and humans

For thousands of years, birds of prey have influenced people, and people have influenced birds of prey. These birds have been admired and worshiped, feared and persecuted. Now more than ever, we must look after them, so that future generations can discover their fascination.

Cave drawings

Humans have envied and admired birds of prey for their powerful flight and extraordinary eyesight. Early humans probably stole food from raptors that had made a successful kill. They would have had no trouble driving the birds away.

During the Ice Age, Paleolithic humans drew eagles on the walls of caves. The eagles may have represented more than a meal; they may have had some religious or magical meaning.

Falcon gods

Falcon gods were common in Egyptian culture more than 3000 years ago. Falcons there were worshiped in temples and made into mummies. Their effortless flight and fantastic eyesight were thought to have supernatural properties. The eye of Horus, the falcon-headed sun god, was engraved on charms and was believed to protect the wearer.

Armies of Ancient Rome also valued the image of an eagle. A symbol of military strength, images of eagles were carried into battle on banners and shields. Even today,

falcons and eagles appear on the crests of many big organizations. Their message: that the business is strong and reliable.

C.M. Dixon

◄ *In Ancient Egypt, a falcon-headed man represented Horus, supreme god of the sun. This story was drawn in about 1250 BC by the scribe (writer) Ani. It is easy to understand how high-flying falcons were thought to be connected with the sun, the gods, and the heavens.*

▼ *An old photograph shows the large number of falcons that were trapped on migration through China. They were hooded to keep them calm and taken to Peking to be sold for falconry.*

Popperfoto

Raptors do not always have such a good image. In the Bible (Leviticus 1: 13–18) several species are listed as unclean, because they eat blood with their food. However, in Exodus, the eagle represents the powerful protection of the Lord.

Protector of Indians

Protection was the supernatural quality that the American Plains Indians gave to birds of prey. To discover their personal protector, the Indians fasted and prayed. If a falcon or eagle appeared to them in a vision, its feathers would be attached to battle shields and used in prayer.

Aboriginal legend

Australian Aborigines used birds of prey in their legends. One tale is about two brothers, Falcon and Eagle, who went hunting. They found some kangaroos in a cave. Eagle went inside, while Falcon guarded the entrance. Eagle sent out the thin kangaroos and kept the fat ones for himself. This angered Falcon, who lit a fire in the cave, blackening the Eagle's feathers. The moral of the story is that you shouldn't be selfish. The story also shows that the Aborigines knew a bit about birds of prey, for eagles are black, and falcons do not like them. The falcons stoop at any eagles that invade their territory.

Useful to man

In prehistoric times, perhaps as early as 4000 years ago, humans began to use hawks to catch food for them. Later, falconry became a sport for recreation. Today it is also used to clear birds from airfields and vineyards.

Hawks can be useful predators of pests. Kestrels eat mice; goshawks eat rabbits; and many raptors eat locusts. Unfortunately hawks sometimes come into conflict with humans when they eat animals we want to eat or those that we value for other reasons.

Too often, hawks are shot when raiding poultry farms, and falcons are destroyed by pigeon-racers. People still have a strange mixture of fear of and fascination for birds of prey. But, more and more, people enjoy raptors and understand that they have their place in nature.

▼ *This beautiful tapestry was made in Germany, in about 1490, to celebrate a marriage. The lady has a hawk on her fist. Nearby another hawk kills a hare, surrounded by the hunting dogs used to flush prey for the hawks. This was the period when falconry was at its most popular; raptors were kept to catch food for the table, and for sport.*

Arabs and falconry

For thousands of years the Arabs have used trained hawks and falcons to catch food. Today, as the Middle East is changed by the oil industry, wealthy Arabs still return to the desert to hunt with falcons. To them, falconry is part of their cultural identity.

Arab falconry

Falconry is the use of a bird of prey, trained by reward, to hunt. In the Middle East it was once a necessity; the prey captured was an important source of food. Now food is no longer a problem, and the camels and horses of earlier hunting expeditions have been replaced by four-wheel-drive vehicles.

Falconry with a hawk

Accipiters (goshawks and sparrowhawks) used to be more popular with Arab falconers, particularly in coastal areas. The sparrowhawk was held in one hand and thrown, like a spear, in the direction of prey. The extra speed gave the hawk an advantage. It could easily catch as many as eight quails in just one hour.

▶ *A young Bedouin is taught falconry, just as his father and grandfather were. For generations, falcons caught food for the Arabs in the harsh desert. Today many wealthy Arabs still return to the desert to hunt with falcons.*

▼ *A French painting from the early nineteenth century shows the excitement of falconry in Algeria. The riders in the background have flushed a shorebird towards two hawks flown together as a "cast". The two take turns to attack.*

Nick Gordon/Ardea London

Hunting expeditions

In winter large groups of men and their falcons head for the desert. Around the campfire they share jokes and stories of the day's hunt and of hunts of old. Their falcons are fed and tethered nearby: Sakers, Peregrines, Lanners, and occasionally Barbary Falcons.

The Saker is their favorite. It can withstand the high desert temperatures and is an aggressive and adaptable hunter. The falconers prefer passage birds—that is, those in their first year, on their first migration. Females, being larger, are more highly prized than males.

Endangered quarry

Traditionally the falconers hunted hares, stone curlews, the Houbara Bustard, and the Arabian Gazelle. Now, sadly, the gazelle has almost disappeared, and the bustard is endangered. Modern vehicles rip up the fragile desert. Falconry continues in the Middle East, but its survival depends on the conservation of prey, habitat, and falcon.

Hans Christain Heap/Planet Earth Pictures

▲ *A Saudi Arabian falconer tends his Saker. For their stamina in the desert heat, Arabs value Sakers highly.*

The thrill of the hunt

Wild raptors are seldom seen making a kill. Falconry is one way people can share in the excitement of the chase. It used to be a necessity to provide meat for the table, but now falconry has become a sport. It is popular in Britain, and parts of America and Europe, but is not permitted in some countries.

Early falconry

Falconry may have begun 4000 years ago, perhaps in China. The earliest record is an Assyrian bas-relief (carving) of about 710 BC. The first written evidence is from Japan in 244 AD.

It is known that trained hawks were used for centuries in northern Africa, the Middle East, and parts of Asia, as a means of catching food. The Mongols carried Golden Eagles on horseback, to hunt wolves and foxes.

Between 500 and 1600 AD the popularity of falconry was at its greatest, in Britain, Europe, and the Islamic world. In Britain during the Middle Ages, social rank played a part in determining which kind of hawk a person could keep. A Gyrfalcon was deemed suitable for a king, a Peregrine Falcon for an earl, a Merlin for a lady, and so on, down to a Sparrowhawk for a priest and a kestrel for a servant. In fact, all sorts of people had hawks, and they were part of everyday life. They were used mainly to hunt for food, but also for pleasure. They were even taken to church.

New ways of hunting

The invention of firearms (guns) and a move towards city living caused a decline in falconry in Europe. It also caused a shift in opinion. Many people began to view hawks as an enemy competing for game, and they shot hawks.

Mike Birkhead/Oxford Scientific Films

◀ *To train a bird of prey takes time and patience. Eventually, a very special relationship can develop between the falconer and the bird.*

▼ *Falconers' birds were frequently lost, but now that doesn't happen as much. Today many falconers put radio-transmitters on their valuable birds. There are now transmitters light enough for the falcon to carry, and receivers and antennae convenient enough for the falconer to carry around.*

Michael Freeman/Bruce Coleman Ltd

Nick Greaves/Planet Earth Pictures

▶ *A falconer's prized Peregrine, with hooded head and jessed legs. The bell on the right leg helps the falconer to find the bird if it disappears from sight into a tree or long grass. The tinkle of the bell gives the falcon away. This falcon's beak is in need of a trim—one of the many little jobs necessary to keep a bird in top condition.*

▼ *The British falconer often prefers to hunt alone and on foot. The falconer's dog flushes game for the falcon, which "waits on" high above and then stoops at the quarry. The stoop is much admired by British and American falconers, but not by the Arabs, who prefer short direct flights.*

Blindfolded
Hoods are like blindfolds. Putting on a well-fitting hood instantly calms an excited or fearful falcon. The hooded falcon sits quietly in the darkness, without jumping around and breaking feathers. Some hoods are so beautifully crafted that they are works of art.

Falconry today
A few falconers kept falconry alive, and since the 1950s several clubs have been formed in Britain and Europe. Falconry has become established in America. Nowadays it is practiced for sport rather than necessity.

A lot of time, patience, and experience is needed to train a bird—plus the expense of housing it and taking it out every day. However, the rewards can be great. Dedicated falconers get great joy from the whole experience of being in wild country, sharing spectacular flights, and feeling part of nature.

Typically, falconers use "shortwings" (goshawks and sparrowhawks) and "longwings" (falcons). Various other hawks and eagles are sometimes trained. Each is suited to a particular type of prey, habitat, and hunting technique.

Trained raptors have been used to scare birds from airfields and keep starlings away from vineyards. Falconry techniques have been used to help breed captive raptors and release them to re-establish wild populations reduced by pesticide poisoning. Some techniques are also useful in the rehabilitation of injured birds.

Glossary

BROOD	All the chicks that hatch from one clutch of eggs.
TO BROOD	To cover the chicks to keep them warm and dry.
CERE	The fleshy bit, where the beak joins the head, in which the nostrils lie. The beak grows continuously (rather like a fingernail) from the cere and wears off at the tip and edges.
CLUTCH	A set of eggs in a nest, laid by one female.
COLONIAL	Roosting, nesting, or hunting in groups.
COURTSHIP	Activities concerned with finding and keeping a mate for breeding. Display flying, bowing, and calling are often part of courtship. In courtship feeding the male offers the female the prey he has caught.
CROP	A sac in the gut just above the breast into which food passes first, after it is swallowed. Food is held there before moving down into the stomach.
EGG TOOTH	A small white projection on the front of a chick's upper beak to help it open the shell at hatching. Usually it drops off a few days after hatching.
EMBRYO	A bird in its earliest stages of development, in the egg.
EYRIE	The nest of a bird of prey.
FALCONRY	Sometimes known as "hawking". To train, by reward, a bird of prey, not necessarily a falcon. The bird flies free and may capture prey.
FLEDGE	To become feathered, or to leave the nest, usually by flying.
FLEDGLING	A young, inexperienced bird that has left the nest. In the case of birds of prey, a fledgling is generally still in the care of its parents.
HABITAT	The type of place where a bird lives, to which it is most suited (e.g. tropical rainforest).
HOOD	In falconry, a leather cap which fits over the head of a bird of prey. It covers the eyes but leaves the beak free. It is shaped carefully so that the leather does not touch the bird's eyes.
HOVER	To flutter in the air above a fixed point.
INCUBATE	To sit on eggs and keep them warm (and moist). Each egg must be kept at the right temperature and humidity for the embryo to develop.
JESSES	Strips of leather that a falconer attaches to the legs of his or her bird to hold the bird onto the falconer's gloved wrist.
MIGRATORY	Birds (and other animals) that make regular seasonal movements from one part of the world to another.
NESTLING	A young bird before it has left the nest.
ORNITHOLOGIST	A scientist who specializes in the study of birds.
PLUMAGE	A bird's feathers.
POPULATION	All the individuals of a species in a particular area or country.
PREY, QUARRY	The animals hunted by a bird of prey.
PRIMARIES	The ten outermost flight feathers in the wing. They are usually longer and narrower than the inner flight feathers, which are called the secondaries.
RAPTOR	A bird of prey; sometimes includes the owls.
RESIDENT	Remaining in or around the same place all year.
ROOST	A regular perch where the raptor rests (and preens) by day or night. It can be in a tree, on a cliff, on the ground among tall grass, in a hollow, etc., and is usually protected from bad weather.
SOAR	To glide along, high in the air, without flapping the wings.
SOLITARY	Roosting, nesting, or hunting alone (or in a pair, comprising a male and a female).
STOOP	A spectacular dive from great height.
TALONS	The claws of birds of prey.
TOMIAL TOOTH	A projection on the upper beak of falcons, bazas, and a few other raptors. It may help with handling prey but is not a true tooth.

List of scientific names

There are about 292 species of birds of prey. Each has two names: a common name and a scientific name. The common name is written in ordinary lettering. It is the everyday name that people use, and it is often different in different parts of the world. For example, the Osprey is sometimes called the Fish Hawk.

The scientific name is always the same for any one species. It is based on Latin and is printed in *italics*. Animals are named according to their relationships with each other. Similar species (types) are grouped into a genus; that is the first part of the scientific name. The second part of the scientific name refers to a particular species. For example, all the true falcons are in the genus *Falco*, but only the Peregrine Falcon is *Falco peregrinus*.

The falcons and hawks in this book are listed below.

COMMON NAME	SCIENTIFIC NAME	COMMON NAME	SCIENTIFIC NAME
Osprey	*Pandion haliaetus*	Cooper's Hawk	*Accipiter cooperii*
Asian Baza	*Aviceda jerdoni*	Northern Goshawk	*Accipiter gentilis*
Crested Baza	*Aviceda subcristata*	Slate-colored Hawk	*Leucopternis schistacea*
Black Baza	*Aviceda leuphotes*	Harris' Hawk	*Parabuteo unicinctus*
Hook-billed Kite	*Chondrohierax uncinatus*	Broad-winged Hawk	*Buteo platypterus*
Western Honey Buzzard	*Pernis apivorus*	Swainson's Hawk	*Buteo swainsoni*
Swallow-tailed Kite	*Elanoides forficatus*	Galapagos Hawk	*Buteo galapagoensis*
Pearl Kite	*Gampsonyx swainsonii*	Red-backed Hawk	*Buteo polyosoma*
White-tailed Kite	*Elanus leucurus*	Zone-tailed Hawk	*Buteo albonatatus*
Black-shouldered Kite	*Elanus caeruleus*	Red-tailed Hawk	*Buteo jamaicensis*
Black-winged Kite	*Elanus notatus*	Eurasian Buzzard	*Buteo buteo*
Letter-winged Kite	*Elanus scriptus*	Ferruginous Hawk	*Buteo regalis*
Snail Kite	*Rostrhamus sociabilis*	Rough-legged Hawk	*Buteo lagopus*
Plumbeous Kite	*Ictinia plumbea*		
Mississippi Kite	*Ictinia mississippiensis*	Striated Caracara	*Phalcoboenus australis*
Red Kite	*Milvus milvus*	African Pygmy Falcon	*Polihierax semitorquatus*
Black Kite	*Milvus migrans*	Black-thighed Falconet	*Microhierax fringillarius*
Whistling Kite	*Haliastur sphenurus*	Bornean Falconet	*Microhierax latifrons*
Brahminy Kite	*Haliastur indus*	American Kestrel	*Falco sparverius*
African Harrier Hawk	*Polyboroides typus*	Old World Kestrel	*Falco tinnunculus*
Madagascar Harrier Hawk	*Polyboroides radiatus*	Mauritius Kestrel	*Falco punctatus*
Eastern Chanting Goshawk	*Melierax poliopterus*	Australian Kestrel	*Falco cenchroides*
Dark Chanting Goshawk	*Melierax metabates*	White-eyed Kestrel	*Falco rupicoloides*
Pale Chanting Goshawk	*Melierax canorus*	Eleonora's Falcon	*Falco eleonorae*
Spotted Harrier	*Circus assimilis*	Sooty Falcon	*Falco concolor*
Northern Harrier	*Circus cyaneus*	Aplomado Falcon	*Falco femoralis*
Montagu's Harrier	*Circus pygargus*	Merlin	*Falco columbarius*
African Marsh Harrier	*Circus ranivorus*	Northern Hobby	*Falco subbuteo*
Brown Goshawk	*Accipiter fasciatus*	Brown Falcon	*Falco berigora*
Variable Goshawk	*Accipiter novaehollandiae*	Gray Falcon	*Falco hypoleucos*
Little Sparrowhawk	*Accipiter minullus*	Prairie Falcon	*Falco mexicanus*
Japanese Sparrowhawk	*Accipiter gularis*	Lanner Falcon	*Falco biarmicus*
Australasian Collared		Saker Falcon	*Falco cherrug*
Sparrowhawk	*Accipiter cirrhocephalus*	Gyrfalcon	*Falco rusticolus*
Eurasian Sparrowhawk	*Accipiter nisus*	Peregrine Falcon	*Falco peregrinus*
Sharp-shinned Hawk	*Accipiter striatus*	Barbary Falcon	*Falco pelegrinoides*

Index